THE ART OF MANAGING FINANCE

David B. Davies

McGRAW-HILL BOOK COMPANY

London · New York · St Louis · San Francisco · Auckland
Bogotá · Caracas · Hamburg · Lisbon · Madrid · Mexico
Milan · Montreal · New Delhi · Panama · Paris · San Juan
São Paulo · Singapore · Sydney · Tokyo · Toronto

Published by
McGRAW-HILL Book Company Europe
Shoppenhangers Road, Maidenhead, Berkshire, England SL6 2QL
Telephone Maidenhead (0628) 23432
Fax 0628 770224

British Library Cataloguing in Publication Data

Davies, David B. (David Basil),
 The art of managing finance   2nd edn.
 I. Title
 658.15
 ISBN 0–07–707441–6

Library of Congress Cataloging in Publication Data

Davies, David B. (David Basil)
 The art of managing finance
 David B. Davies. — 2nd ed.
  p. cm.
 Includes bibliographical references and index.
 ISBN 0–07–707441–6 :
 1. Business enterprises—Finance. 2. Corporations–Finance.
 I. Title.
 HG4026.D378   1992   91–40799
 658.16—dc20   CIP

1234 CL 95432

Typeset by TecSet Ltd, Wallington, Surrey
and printed and bound in England by Clays Ltd, St Ives plc

CONTENTS

To Ann
With thanks for her help and support

ONE

SCOPE OF FINANCIAL MANAGEMENT

Any business must have money if it is to survive. Surprisingly the great majority of businesses are profitable when they fail. In the United Kingdom 75–80 per cent cease to trade because they lack money and not because they are unprofitable. This book sets out to explain the difference between liquidity, the ability of an organization to pay its way, and profitability, the return on investment. The balance sheet, income statement and cash budget as the main financial statements are fully explained; once these are understood the ways in which the finances employed in an organization may be managed are discussed. Contrary to general belief, financial management is an art and not an exact science, which explains why many people are good at it but some bad. The available techniques can be learned but their application depends on the time, place and situation in which they are to be applied and on the person applying them.

Accounting has developed from its original role of stewardship, when it was used to reassure merchants that their goods were not being stolen, to its present purpose of not only maintaining stewardship of the property of an organization but also as an aid to management in planning, decision making and control. Accounting has come a long way but it still does not replace the managers who make decisions based on the information that is available.

Prior to the twentieth century, financial accounting with its emphasis on past events, enabled a report to be prepared on the profit that had been made or the loss incurred by an organization in a financial period, generally a year. This, together with its ability to account for the resources of an organization, provided owners/managers with the information that they felt was needed. The twentieth century, particularly since the end of the Second World War, has been a period of accelerating growth and change. Financial accounts, which provide largely historical information, are still essential but no longer sufficient to meet the needs of owners/managers. To enable business to survive, plans have to be prepared to cope with changing needs and the plans themselves must be capable of modification. This led to the development of management accounting, which enables owners/managers to plan the course of their organizations and control their operations more effectively.

This book covers financial accounting, which is largely for external users, although much information is also provided internally through the key ratios that are discussed later. It also describes management accounting with its emphasis on providing the right information at the right time for the right people. It is no good waiting until the end of the financial year to discover that your plan started to go wrong 11 months ago. To be useful information must be obtained quickly and accurately and be transmitted to the person most directly concerned. In order for this to be done information must be provided regularly and quickly. Financial analysis should be carried out at least monthly and if possible weekly. Modern management information systems enable this to be done and data can be transmitted electronically and instantaneously to the relevant manager. If plans are to work, and control is to be maintained, management must be able to respond to changing conditions as they arise.

1.1   FLOW OF FUNDS

The diagram (Figure 1.1), which resembles a water system, represents a business and the money circulating in it. To start any business funds must first of all be obtained. The money may come from the owner's savings, in which case it is equity capital. It may be borrowed for periods of five years or more (long-term loan), or for between one and four years (short-term loan). Having obtained the money that is needed to start a business it has to be managed. The type of business will have been decided before the finance is obtained, so the next major decision may be what premises are to be used and, if it is a manufacturing concern, what plant and machinery are needed. These items are known as fixed assets and require a heavy outlay of money. The next decision is which supplier to use to provide the items that are needed to manufacture the product and what credit can be obtained. These items, once obtained, become the stock of raw materials. Decisions will have to be made on the number of people that are to be employed, the number of telephones to be installed and a multiplicity of other matters, all of which require financing.

Once these decisions have been made it will be necessary to implement them and start the manufacturing process as soon as possible. Until the business has a product for which there is a demand and has succeeded in selling that product, there will be a continuous drain from the pool of money and if the business finances are not properly managed it may well disappear altogether. The 'pumps' in the chart represent the points at which good management can speed up the whole process. The successful integration of people and materials requires good management and the more effectively this is done the better for the business.

There is a leak of resources through the tap at the pool of stock. This is a controllable leak and its size depends upon the success or otherwise with which the raw materials are managed. If store facilities are poor and the storeman is not very interested in his job the leak will be large due to breakages, obsolete items, rust and pilfering. The loss will be minimized by a good system of stores control backed by well-trained staff.

During and immediately following the production process there are two other 'pools' in which the resources employed in a business become trapped. These are work in progress

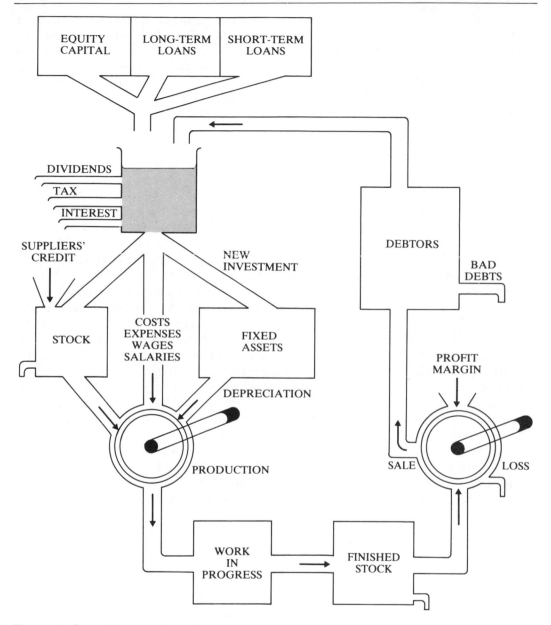

Figure 1.1 Chart of Business Funds Flow

(WIP) and finished stock. In even the most successfully managed businesses there will be at the end of each accounting period some items that are between the raw material and finished goods stage. Management would like all items to be produced as quickly as possible but as things take time to be made, work in progress can never be eliminated. It should not, however, be allowed to build up to an unnecessarily high level. There are problems too in deciding how work in progress should be valued and the system necessary to keep track of it has to be detailed. Finished stock should be sold and delivered as quickly as possible, although in some cases where the demand for the goods is seasonal it may be necessary to have facilities to hold quite a lot of finished stock. Toy manufacture, where the bulk of the sales takes place at Christmas, is one example of this. The lack of resources at the finished stock stage can be serious unless a good system of stores control is employed. The loss can be due to pilfering, obsolescence, breakages and general deterioration. Stock levels in this country used to be much higher in the manufacturing sector than in America, Germany and Japan, but the destocking brought about by the present recession has lowered them quite dramatically. Indeed the *just in time* method of stock control attempts to eliminate the need to hold raw material stocks at all.

The next point at which good management can greatly improve the resources available to the business is by selling and distributing the finished goods as quickly as possible and obtaining the money from the firm's customers in the shortest possible time. There may be a loss at the time of sale, which good procedures can largely eliminate, caused by damage, pilferage and below-standard items that are returned, as well as items incorrectly delivered. It is here that the greatest potential loss occurs, that of bad debts (people who take delivery of goods but do not pay for them). Most business is conducted on credit and with the difficulty in obtaining sales, credit has become easier to obtain. It is one element in the marketing mix and its terms depend on many factors, including custom and practice of the trade and the pressures on the company to make a sale. Nearly all businesses suffer from bad debts, and, in order to keep them to a minimum, an efficient system of credit control is essential. The practice of factoring your debts, which entails employing a third person who obtains your money for you for a fee, is widespread in America and growing in this country. It has the advantage of giving the business money to use more quickly than would otherwise be the case. The criticism most usually levied against it is that it destroys the special relationship between the organization and its customers.

The money having been collected from the customers is now replacing some of that used in starting the business, but the 'taps' of dividends, tax and interest have to be considered. Shareholders' dividends can be paid only out of profits so if no profits have been made no dividends will be expected. If profits have been made dividends may be paid at the discretion of the owners but it is not a requirement. If a business is continually making a profit but refuses to pay dividends without good reason it will find it difficult to obtain money from the public when it next needs it. Interest has to be paid whether the business is profitable or not, which means that businesses have to ensure that they do not borrow so much that they cannot afford the interest charges. Recent examples of this include British and Commonwealth and Brent Walker. The amount of interest to be paid depends on the size and terms of borrowing which good management can ensure remain within the capability of the business. Tax is chargeable on profits but is at a minimum in the early years of manufacturing businesses, because of capital allowances, as well as when any large capital investment programme has been undertaken.

The amount of money that a business has to enable it to operate until more money has been received is called its working capital, the difference between the capital it will have available within the next four or five months and what it will have to pay within the same period. It may need enough working capital to keep it going for five months before it receives any further resources.

This may be broken down as:

Obtaining raw materials	4 weeks	
Manufacturing process	4 weeks	
Held in stock	4 weeks	These periods are for example only and
Collect money from customer	8 weeks	will vary from industry to industry
Total	20 weeks	

All this time the costs, expenses, wages and salaries have to be met. It is for this reason that it is important to ensure that the working capital and other financial resources of the business are properly managed. The following chapters demonstrate how this may be achieved.

BALANCE SHEET

The balance sheet is a map, or photograph, of a business's financial position on a specific date. It refers *only* to that date and covers no period of time. It shows where the business has obtained its resources, and the purpose to which they have been put at that date. The balance sheet must always balance because no business can ever use more or less resources than it has obtained.

The business and its owner are separate entities, and because of this the balance sheet tells us something about the business but *nothing at all* about the owner.

2.1 CAPITAL

The capital of a business is the sum of the resources for which business has to account to the owner, i.e., if a man started a business with life savings of £5,000 which he paid into the business bank account and his own car valued at £3,000 to be used solely in the business, the bank sheet on the first day of business would be:

Uses	£	Sources	£
Motor vehicle	3,000	Capital	8,000
Bank balance	5,000		
	8,000		8,000

The resources have been obtained from the owner. The uses to which they have been put are a motor vehicle and business bank account. Another way of describing the sources of the resources of the business is as liabilities. The capital of the business is a liability to the owner, i.e. in certain circumstances, like business failure, it is due to be paid by the business to the owner. The 'uses' to which the resources have been put could also be described as assets, i.e., the motor vehicle and the bank balance belong to the business, and are assets used in the operation of the business.

The business would not survive if it remained in its present form. In order to function it needs premises and some commodity with which to deal or service to offer. This commodity in which a business deals is called stock. The business buys premises for £14,000 and stock for £1,000, both of which it pays for in cash. It borrows £10,000 from the bank. The balance sheet would now look like this.

Uses (assets)	£	Sources (liabilities)	£
Fixed assets:		Capital	8,000
Premises	14,000	Loan	10,000
Motor vehicle	3,000		
	17,000		
Current assets:			
Stock	1,000		
	18,000		18,000

The capital remains unaltered but the uses to which it has been put have changed.

2.2 FIXED ASSETS

Fixed assets are those that are retained in the business for several accounting years and are used within the business over their useful life to enable it to operate. In the example, premises and motor vehicles are fixed assets because the business is retaining and using them. However, if the business traded in motor vehicles or premises only those retained by the business for its own use would be fixed assets, the remainder would be 'stock'.

2.3 CURRENT ASSETS

Current assets are those that are usually consumed by the business in the course of one accounting year. The stock of the business would normally be sold and replaced at least once in an accounting year, and therefore it is a current asset. The business has been established but needs to start trading. The owner sells stock that cost £500 on credit for £900. The effect on the balance sheet is:

Uses (assets)	£	£	Sources (liabilities)	£	
Fixed assets:			Capital	8,000	
Premises	14,000		Reserves:		
Motor vehicle	3,000	17,000	Retained profit	400	
Current assets:			Owner's equity		8,400
Stock	500		Loan		10,000
Debtor	900	1,400			
		18,400			18,400

2.4 PROFIT

The profit of £400 is shown as a source of funds and is added to the reserves which are profits that are kept in the business. It is due to the owner by the business. The profit is the excess of the selling price over the cost price of the stock (£900 – £500). **Note that although the business has made a profit of £400 it has no cash. Profit does not equal cash. Neither do reserves!**

2.5 DEBTOR

A debtor is any institution or person owing money to the business for goods or services received from the business. It is therefore both an asset of the business, because it can be called upon to pay what it owes, and a use of funds because the debtor has received benefits for which no payment has yet been made.

In order to expand further his business operations the owner feels it necessary to extend the credit facilities that he is able to offer his customers, and improve his premises internally with some filing cabinets and general office equipment. To do this he obtains a further loan of £6,000 which will be repayable in five years' time. The money is used to buy furniture and equipment for £4,000 and stock of £1,000. The balance sheet redrawn will be:

Uses (assets)	£	£	Sources (liabilities)	£	£
Fixed assets:			Capital	8,000	
Premises	14,000		Reserves:		
Furniture and			Retained profit	400	
equipment	4,000			———	
Motor vehicle	3,000	21,000	Owner's equity		8,400
	———		Loan		16,000
Current assets:					
Stock	1,500				
Debtor	900				
Cash	1,000	3,400			
	———	———			———
		24,400			24,400
		═══			═══

Furniture and equipment is a fixed asset because it will be retained in the running of the business for several years.

Cash is a current asset because it will be very quickly used in the normal course of business events.

Loan is a long-term liability and so comes between capital and reserves which are permanent, and current liabilities, which are sources that are repaid in the course of one financial period.

The business is ready to operate at full throttle so it obtains £4,000 worth of stock on credit, and sells stock that cost £2,000 for £5,500; of this £2,500 represents cash sales and £3,000 credit sales. The balance sheet shows:

Uses (assets)	£	£	Sources (liabilities)	£	£
Fixed assets:			Capital	8,000	
Premises	14,000		Reserves:		
Furniture and			Retained profit	3,900	
equipment	4,000			———	
Motor vehicle	3,000	21,000	Owner's equity		11,900
	———		Loan		16,000
Current assets:			Current liabilities:		
Stock	3,500		Creditors		4,000
Debtors	3,900				
Cash	3,500	10,900			
	———				———
		31,900			31,900

The *profit* figure of £3,900 is made up of the £400 previous profit, plus the profit on this sale of £3,500 (£5,500 – £2,000).

The *stock* figure of £3,500 is made up of the £1,500 previous stock plus the stock purchased of £4,000, minus the stock sold which cost the business £2,000 to buy (£1,500 + £4,000 – £2,000 = £3,500).

The *debtor* figure of £3,900 is made up of the £900 previous debtors plus the £3,000 owing for stock sold.

The *cash* figure of £3,500 is made up of the £1,000 previous cash balance plus the £2,500 received from cash sales.

The businessman needs extra resources to take full advantage of an expanding market. He is also a little nervous of the liabilities and so he decides to convert his business to a *private limited company*, with an authorized and issued capital of £30,000 in £1 ordinary shares. He issues shares at par (that is a £1 share for £1) as follows:

11,900 for the owner's interest or capital in his own name to the owner (himself)
 3,100 for the goodwill in his own name to the owner
 5,000 for cash in his own name to the owner
10,000 Every Finance Company Ltd for cash

The costs of company formation were paid by the owner and confirmed by the company after incorporation. The costs were:

		£
Capital duty 50p per cent of £30,000		150
Conveyance duty		100
Legal, printing and postage costs		80
		——
		330

Before the new balance sheet can be drawn up the new cash balance must be calculated:

	£	£
Receipts:		
Opening cash	3,500	
Cash for his own shares	5,000	
Cash from finance company	10,000	18,500
Payments:		
Formation expenses shown above		330
Cash balance in hand		18,170

Business Ltd
Balance Sheet as at Day 0

	£	£		£
Goodwill		3,100	Authorized capital:	
Fixed assets:			30,000 £1 ordinary shares	30,000
Premises	14,000			
Furniture and			Issued capital:	
equipment	4,000		30,000 ordinary shares	30,000
Motor vehicle	3,000	21,000	Loan	16,000
Current assets:				
Stock	3,500		Current liabilities:	
Debtors	3,900		Creditors	4,000
Cash	18,170			
Preliminary expenses	330	25,900		
		50,000		50,000

Ordinary shares are shares that carry voting rights and the person or group with the most controls the business. In this case the owner has retained control with 20,000 out of the 30,000 shares issued.

Authorized capital is the amount authorized to be issued in the memorandum of association.*

Goodwill represents the value that a prospective purchaser would be prepared to pay for the business over its book value, because its contacts enable it to make more profit than an entirely new business in the same field could make. It appears in the balance sheet only when more has been received for a business than the book value of the assets acquired.

Preliminary expenses are carried in the balance sheet until the owner of the business decides to write them off against profits. They are shown as an asset because the business gets the benefit of them over its whole life. They are the formation expenses shown above.

The business buys £30,000 of stock. It pays £15,000 cash and gets the other half on credit. It sells £20,000 of it for £40,000, half cash and half on credit. The balance sheet now shows:

*The memorandum of association gives the name of the company, where the registered office is to be situated and the objects of the company.

Business Ltd
Balance sheet as at Day 1

	£	£		£	£
Goodwill		3,100	Authorized capital:		
Fixed assets:			30,000 £1		
Premises	14,000		ordinary shares		30,000
Furniture and			Issued capital:		———
equipment	4,000		30,000 £1		
Motor vehicle	3,000	21,000	ordinary shares	30,000	
	———		Reserves:		
Current assets:			Retained profits	20,000	
Stock	13,500			———	
Debtors	23,900		Equity interest		50,000
Cash	23,170		Loan		16,000
			Current liabilities:		
Preliminary expenses	330	60,900	Creditors		19,000
	———				———
		85,000			85,000
		═══			═══

Reserves in this case consist solely of retained profits. That is, profits that have been retained in the business in order to strengthen it rather than distributed to the shareholders as dividends. **Reserves do not represent cash.** In studying company balance sheets you will see that it is possible to have very large reserves but very little money. This is because reserves are simply another source of the resources that are being used on the assets side of the balance sheet to buy premises, equipment, stocks or some other assets which may well include, but will not solely be, cash.

The business buys a further £20,000 of stock for cash and sells stock that cost £30,000 on credit for £60,000. A general reserve of £20,000 is created by the business and the preliminary expenses are written off. The balance sheet becomes:

Business Ltd
Balance sheet as at Day 2

	£	£		£	£
Goodwill		3,100	Authorized capital:		
Fixed assets:			30,000 £1 ordinary shares		30,000
Premises	14,000				———
Furniture and			Issued capital:		
equipment	4,000		30,000 £1 ordinary shares		30,000
Motor vehicle	3,000	21,000	Reserves:		
	———		Retained profit	29,670	
Current assets:			General reserve	20,000	49,670
Stock	3,500			———	
Debtors	83,900		Owner's equity		79,670
Cash	3,170	90,570	Loan		16,000
	———		Current liabilities:		
			Creditors		19,000
					———
		114,670			114,670
		═══			═══

The *stock* figure is arrived at in the following way:

	£
Opening stock (previous balance sheet)	13,500
Purchases	20,000
	33,500
Less Sales at cost	30,000
	3,500

The *cash* figure is calculated as follows:

	£
Opening cash (previous balance sheet)	23,170
Less Cash purchases	20,000
	3,170

The *debtors'* figure consists of previous debtors £23,900 plus this period's credit sales of £60,000.

The *retained profits* consist of:

	£	£
Opening balance (previous balance sheet)		20,000
Add This period's profit		30,000
		50,000
Deduct:		
Transfer to general reserve	20,000	
Preliminary expenses written off	330	20,330
		29,670

Notice that the reserves are undistributed **profit** and usually **not cash**. The balance sheet now has reserves of £49,670 but cash of only £3,170. The preliminary expenses have been written off against profits with no effect on cash.

All the balance sheets shown so far have been in the traditional two-sided form. Most published balance sheets are in the narrative or vertical form as this format is said to be easier to understand. The balance sheet of Business Ltd on Day 2 can be redrawn in the vertical form as follows:

Business Ltd
Balance sheet as at Day 2

	£	£
Goodwill		3,100
Fixed assets:		
Premises	14,000	
Furniture and equipment	4,000	
Motor vehicle	3,000	21,000
Current assets:		
Stock	3,500	
Debtors	83,900	
Cash	3,170	
	90,570	
Less Current liabilities:		
Creditors	19,000	
WORKING CAPITAL		71,570
NET CAPITAL EMPLOYED		95,670

		£
Financed by:		
30,000 £1 ordinary shares		30,000
Reserves:		
Retained profit	29,670	
General reserve	20,000	49,670
Equity interest		79,670
Loan		16,000
		95,670

The vertical form of balance sheet readily gives more information, without the need for calculation, than the two-sided form.

Working capital and *net capital employed* are both visible at a glance in the vertical form, but must be calculated in the two-sided balance sheet. *Equity interest* is that part of the business belonging to the owners.

The importance of having sufficient working capital to enable your business to operate while it awaits receipts from its activities cannot be overemphasized, although it should be remembered that to have too much is as bad as having too little. The objective is to decide what a sensible level is for the particular business and endeavour to maintain it at that level.

BALANCE SHEET QUESTIONS

2.1 Evans has decided to start his own business. After careful thought he decided to open a shop selling video cassettes. He has £20,000 which he obtained by increasing the mortgage on his house. The £20,000 is paid into the business bank account. Draw up the business balance sheet as at 30 September, the day on which he paid the money into the business bank account.

2.2 On 4 October he rents shop premises at a monthly rental of £500 payable in arrears. He also buys cassettes for £4,000 with which he intends to stock the shop. He pays for the cassettes. His mother will work in the shop and is to receive wages of £50 per week. Draw up his business balance as at 4 October.

2.3 He buys a further £10,000 worth of cassettes and cassette players on 7 October for which he will pay at the end of the month. On the same date he sells cassettes that cost him £300 for £400 cash. Draw up his business balance sheet as at 7 October.

2.4 On 8 October he sells cassettes that cost him £500 for £666. Cash to be received in 30 days. Draw up his business balance sheet at that date.

2.5 He pays his mother her wages of £50 on 11 October. Draw up his business balance sheet at that date.

2.6 Business is going well, and so on 14 October he decided to buy the lease of his premises for £25,000. To enable him to do so he has a bank loan of £15,000 and pays cash. Draw up his balance sheet at the date.

ANSWERS
2.1

Balance sheet as at 30 September

	£		£
Current assets:		Capital	20,000
Bank	20,000		
	20,000		20,000

Comments The fact that Evans has increased the mortgage on his house does not appear in the balance sheet since this is a private transaction between Evans and the lender. The balance sheet tells us a little about the business but nothing at all about the owner. The business and its owner are entirely separate entities.

2.2

Balance sheet as at 4 October

	£		£
Current assets:		Capital	20,000
Stock	4,000		
Bank	16,000		
	20,000		20,000

Comments His mother is to work in the shop and will receive £50 per week. This is to happen in the future and does not appear in this balance sheet. If he owed his mother her wages now they would appear as a current liability; £50 is not large enough to warrant a note at the foot of the business sheet, but if Evans had entered into a contract for £50,000 it would be significant enough to be shown as a note. The same argument applies to the rent that does not become due until the end of the month.

2.3

Balance sheet as at 7 October

	£		£
Current assets:		Capital	20,000
Stock	13,700	Reserves:	
Bank	16,400	Profit	100
		Current liabilities:	
		Creditor	10,000
	30,100		30,100

Comments He owes £10,000 for the cassettes that he has received and has made a profit of £100 which goes into reserves.

2.4

Balance sheet as at 8 October

	£		£
Current assets:		Capital	20,000
Stock	13,200	Reserves:	
Debtors	666	Profit	266
Bank	16,400	Current liabilities:	
		Creditors	10,000
	30,266		30,266

Comments He is owed £666 for the cassettes and so debtors appear in the balance sheet and additional profit is added to the reserves.

2.5

Balance sheet as at 11 October

	£		£
Current assets:		Capital	20,000
Stock	13,200	Reserves:	
Debtors	666	Profit	216
Bank	16,350	Current liabilities:	
		Creditors	10,000
	30,216		30,216

Comments The payment of the wages to his mother reduces the bank balance and the profit.

2.6

Balance sheet as at 14 October

	£	£		£
Fixed assets:			Capital:	20,000
Premises		25,000	Reserves:	
Current assets:			Profit	216
Stock	13,200		Loan	15,000
Debtors	666		Current liabilities:	
Bank	6,350	20,216	Creditors	10,000
		45,216		45,216

Comments The bank loan is assumed to be for more than five years and so appears as a long-term liability between reserves and current liabilities. Evans has a fixed asset premises and his bank balance has been reduced by £10,000.

It would be good practice to redraw each of the balance sheets for Evans's business in the vertical form. That for 14 October would become:

Balance sheet as at 14 October

	£	£	£
Fixed assets:			
Premises			25,000
Current assets:			
Stock	13,200		
Debtors	666		
Bank	6,350	20,216	
Deduct Current liabilities:			
Creditors		10,000	
WORKING CAPITAL			10,216
NET CAPITAL EMPLOYED			35,216
Financed by:			
Capital		20,000	
Reserves			
Retained profit		216	
Loan		15,000	
			35,216

THREE

INCOME STATEMENT

An income statement is used to determine the profit a business has made or the loss it has incurred over a trading period. Trading, profit and loss accounts, revenue account, and receipts and payments account are other names used for the income statement. Usually a trading period is taken as one year, but these accounts will be more useful if they are prepared more frequently, i.e., half-yearly, quarterly, or monthly.

The income statement collects together revenue items of income and expense, that is, items that are largely discharged in the financial period and are not held in their present form by the company, nor involve the company in any lasting commitment. In collecting the items for inclusion in the income statement certain accounting principles are followed to ensure comparison is possible between different accounting periods. The main principles are shown below.

3.1 DISTINCTION BETWEEN CAPITAL AND REVENUE EXPENDITURES

Revenue expenditure has an immediate and single impact on profit; examples are wages, rent and rates, heat and light, and postage. Capital expenditure has a lasting impact on the business as it normally results in the acquisition of an asset that will be employed within the business for the purpose of earning resources over several years. Because of this it would not be fair to charge the whole cost of the new capital asset to one accounting period, and so an attempt is made to spread the cost over the accounting periods that will benefit from its use. This annual charge for the use of an asset is called depreciation, and that is the only way that capital expenditure affects profit. Examples of capital expenditure are purchases of plant and machinery, fixtures and fittings, land and buildings, and vehicles.

3.2 PRINCIPLE OF CONSERVATISM

It is considered to be good business practice to provide for all anticipated losses, but ignore any anticipated gains until they are actually realized. This is exactly the principle applied by accountants when they prepare the annual accounts. An example of this is the valuation of stock which is always the lower of cost or current market price. Any rise in price since purchase is ignored until the stock is sold, when the selling price contributes to income.

3.3 PRINCIPLE OF CONSISTENCY

In order to facilitate comparison between one accounting period and another the accounts must be prepared on a consistent basis. Once the method of depreciating a fixed asset has been decided upon, it must be adhered to over the whole life of that asset.

3.4 GOING CONCERN CONCEPT

Balance sheets are prepared on the assumption that the business is going to continue, and the assets are valued on the basis of cost, not what they could be sold for if the business were to fail.

An example of an income statement is:

Business Ltd
Income statement
(trading and profit and loss account)
for the year ending 30 November 19--

	£	£
Sales		80,000
Cost of sales (cost of goods sold):		
Opening stock	5,000	
Add Purchases	100,000	
	105,000	
Deduct Closing stock	45,000	
Cost of sales		60,000
Gross profit		20,000
Administrative and selling expenses:		
Wages	8,000	
Advertising	1,000	
Rates	2,000	
Light and heat	500	
General expenses	500	
Depreciation	1,700	
Bank charges	200	13,900
		6,100

Corporation tax ⎫ These entries depend on the rate of corporation tax and necessary
Net profit after tax ⎭ adjustments.

Sales £80,000   This is the *total* sales figure for the financial year whether the money has been received or not. The figure can be obtained by adding all your sales invoices for the financial year.

Opening stock £5,000   This will have been obtained from a physical count of your stock at the end of the previous financial year and the value put on the stock held.

Purchases £100,000   This is the total of goods purchased during the year, whether or not you have paid for them. This figure can be obtained by totalling all your purchase invoices for the financial year.

Closing stock £45,000   This will be obtained from a physical count of your stock at the end of the financial year with which you are dealing, and a value being put on the stock held.

Gross profit   This represents the difference between the cost price of the goods that you have sold and their selling price (£80,000 – £60,000).

Wages £8,000   This represents total wages for the year and can be obtained from the weekly pay schedules.

Advertising £1,000   This is obtained from bills received or contracts entered into.

Rates £2,000   This is obtained from the rate accounts received from the local authority. It is important to remember that only the part of the rates that relate to *this* financial year go in the income statement. The balance overpaid or underpaid will appear in the balance sheet.

Light and heat £500   This can be obtained from the electricity bills relating to the financial year. Any that relate to any other financial year are excluded from the income statement.

General expenses £500   These are obtained from bills paid for stationery and from the postage book for stamps used on postage.

Depreciation £1,700   This will be obtained as a result of a managerial (or owner's) decision at the time the asset is acquired. Depreciation is a rent or charge for the use of a fixed asset. If a machine costing £10,000 has an anticipated scrap value of £2,000 and is expected to last eight years, then the depreciation charged in each year would be £1,000, calculated by using the following formula (which is one of several available).

$$\frac{\text{Cost} - \text{scrap (or resale value)}}{\text{Number of years useful life}} = \frac{£10,000 - £2,000}{8} = £1,000 \text{ p.a.}$$

Of the three facts used in the calculation only one is known, that is the cost. The other two—life and scrap value—are estimates; as a result depreciation is rarely, if ever, completely accurate. But it is an attempt to spread capital outlay over all the accounting periods that benefit from it. The depreciation of £1,700 was arrived at by:

	£
1. Depreciating the premises in Business Ltd balance sheet by 5 per cent i.e., $\frac{5}{100} \times 14,000$	700
2. Depreciating the furniture and equipment by 10 per cent, i.e., $\frac{10}{100} \times 4,000$	400
3. Depreciating the vehicle by 20 per cent, i.e., $\frac{20}{100} \times 3,000$	600
	1,700

Bank charges £200 These would be obtained from the bank statement.

3.5 INCOME STATEMENT FOR A MANUFACTURING CONCERN

If the business is in manufacturing (as opposed to the retail or service sectors) it will be necessary to prepare a manufacturing account or statement in which all costs of manufacture are collected. The manufacturing statement is part of the income statement and comes at the start of it. When the manufacturing statement is included, the income statement summarizes costs and profits at different levels:

1. Cost of goods made
2. Gross profit
3. Net profit

which is illustrated below:

Manufacturing Business Ltd
Income statement
(manufacturing, trading and profit and loss account)
for the year ending 30 November 19--

	£	£
Cost of material used:		
Opening stock of raw materials	20,000	
Add Purchases of raw materials	70,000	
	90,000	
Deduct Closing stock of raw materials	40,000	
Raw materials used		50,000
Manufacturing labour		20,000
PRIME OR DIRECT COST OF GOODS MADE		70,000
Indirect manufacturing costs:		
Labour (supervisors and cleaning staff)	5,000	
Heat and light of factory or workshop	2,000	
Rent and rates of factory or workshop	10,000	
Depreciation of factory/workshop equipment and machinery	8,000	
General manufacturing expenses	3,000	28,000
		98,000
Add Opening work in progress (WIP)		3,000
		101,000
Deduct Closing work in progress (WIP)		1,000
FACTORY COST OF GOODS MADE		100,000

	£	£
Sales		180,000
Cost of sales (cost of goods sold):		
Opening stock of finished goods	5,000	
Add Factory cost of goods made	100,000	
	105,000	
Deduct Closing stock of finished goods	45,000	
Cost of sales		60,000
Gross Profit		120,000
Administrative and selling expenses:		
Wages	8,000	
Advertising	1,000	
Rates	2,000	
Light and heat	500	
General expenses	500	
Depreciation	1,200	
Bank charges	200	13,400
NET PROFIT BEFORE TAX		£106,600

Corporation tax } These entries depend on the rate of corporation tax and the
Net profit after tax necessary adjustments.

We have three different types of stock which enter the profit calculation at different times:

1. *Raw material stock*. This is calculated by counting the stock of unworked materials that have been bought in and valuing it.
2. *Work in progress (WIP)*. This is calculated by counting the stock of items started but not yet completed. It is extremely difficult to arrive at an accurate figure for this item as it must include a value for both the labour and the materials so far used in the manufacture of the partly finished items as well as other costs.
3. *Finished goods stock*. This is calculated by counting the finished goods and valuing them. It is the stock of goods that is ready for sale.

Raw material purchased This item is calculated by totalling the purchase invoices or orders.

Manufacturing labour This is calculated by totalling the hours on the time sheets or cards, and multiplying them by the appropriate hourly rate. It will equal payment of wages.

Prime or direct cost of goods made This consists of cost items that alter with the volume of output. They are the ones that management can most easily control and should be closely watched.

Indirect labour This is difficult to calculate accurately unless the staff spend their whole time in the workshop, in which case their whole wage will be charged to the manufacturing section. In other cases some sort of apportionment will have to be made, usually on a time basis.

Indirect manufacturing costs   This consists of cost items that do not alter with the volume of output, but are fixed in the short term as a matter of business policy. Little can be done about rent, rates or depreciation in the short term, and so not much time should be spent on controlling them. In long term planning, however, they can have a significant impact and management must be aware of the need to control them.

Heat and light   This item is difficult to calculate unless the workshop is separately metered, in which case the total of the bills will give the figure required. In other cases the cost would be apportioned accordingly to floor area.

Rent and rates   Rent and rates are difficult to calculate unless the workshop is separately assessed. In other cases the charge relating to the workshop should be calculated on the basis of floor area.

Depreciation of machinery and factory or workshop equipment
This will be calculated on the basis of

$$\frac{(Cost - Residual\ value)}{Estimated\ life}$$

General manufacturing expenses   This item is calculated by totalling the miscellaneous invoices for such items as telephones, postage and cleaning materials.

Factory cost of goods made   This is used instead of *purchases* in the gross profit or 'trading' section of the income statement.

The income statement will reveal how much profit or loss an undertaking has made in an accounting period but it will not show the change in the cash balance. **Profit is not equal to increase in cash** and this may be illustrated as follows. Suppose a business has revenues of £50,000 and expenses of £40,000 then the profit will be:

	£
Revenue	50,000
Expenses	40,000
Profit	10,000

Now if the revenue is made up of cash sales £20,000, credit sales £30,000 and the expenses consist of cash purchases £25,000, credit purchases £15,000, then the effect on the cash balance will be:

	£
Receipts	20,000
Payments	25,000
Cash outflow	5,000

A profit of £10,000 has resulted in a deterioration in the cash position of £5,000.

This illustrates how it is that so many profitable organizations fail. They may have poor credit control and eventually run out of money or they may be 'over-trading'—that is growing too rapidly for the resources of the organization to be able to meet the demands put on them. The next chapter suggests a way in which the business can monitor its cash position.

INCOME STATEMENT QUESTIONS
Tom Smith—Barrow boy

3.1   Smith has £3,000 available for starting a business. He decides to become a barrow boy and buys a barrow costing £832, estimated two-year life, and scales costing £208, estimated four-year life.

During the first four weeks he buys second-grade fruit for cash costing £1,500 out of his original fund. After the four weeks he has £2,300 left of his takings after paying out:

	£
Rent of yard	45(£15 per week)
Weekend help	60
Obstruction fines	80

At the end of the four weeks he owes £15 rent and has fruit unsold which cost £100. He considers half to be still saleable.

In order to determine how much he can spend on personal living costs, he asks you to calculate his first four weeks' profit from his business.

3.2   Smith starts his second four weeks' operation with:

	£
One week's rent owing	15
Stock of saleable fruit in hand which cost	50
Cash in hand	2,760
One barrow and one pair of scales	

During the second four weeks he buys fruit for cash to the value of £2,000.

He gives his wife £200 housekeeping money in accordance with his accountant friend's advice.

He takes out a loss of profits insurance policy in case of personal illness at the beginning of the period, payable in advance at an annual premium of £104.

Other payments are:

	£
Rent	45(3 weeks)
Fines	150
Weekend help	60
Cash takings for month	2,800

Closing stock of fruit valued at cost price is £120, half of which is in good condition and half of which he thinks will only fetch £40 (two-thirds of cost).

What is his profit for the second period, his cash balance and financial position at the end of the second period? His wife says she requires more housekeeping money. Can he afford to give it to her?

3.3   Smith starts his third four weeks' operation with:

	£
Two weeks' rent owing	30
Stock of saleable fruit	100
Cash in hand	3,001
Insurance paid in advance	96
One barrow and one pair of scales	

During the four-week period he buys fruit for cash to the value of £2,500.

He decides he can afford to give his wife more housekeeping, and so gives her £450, keeping the balance of the money in the business.

Other payments are:

	£
Rent	75 (5 weeks)
Fines (nil but one prosecution is pending, the current obstruction fines being imposed are £25)	NIL
Weekend help	60
Cash takings for the month	3,300

Sale of the barrow realized £500 on the last day of the period. He purchased a motor van for delivery purposes, also on the last day, for £3,003. Stock of fruit at the end of the period £200 valued at cost.

What is Smith's profit for the period? Was there a profit or loss on the sale of the barrow? What is his financial position at the end of the period?

3.4   Smith starts his fourth four weeks' operation with:

	£
One week's rent owing	15
Stock of saleable fruit which cost	200
Cash in hand	713
Insurance paid in advance	88
Provision for pending fine	25
One motor van and one pair of scales	

His wife feels that £450 housekeeping money is not sufficient and despite his protestations of the need to plough more money back into the business, Smith has to give her £500.

At the magistrates' court he is fined £20 in respect of the outstanding case of obstruction.

During the first week he commences a delivery round on a new estate and enlarges his range of goods to include fresh vegetables. He expects his van to remain in use for two years and it will then have a scrap value of £793.

He arranges a credit account for the purchase of supplies.

His transactions for the period are:

	£
Total cash purchases	1,500
Total purchases on credit	2,500
Cash takings	3,500

Sales to friends living on the estate, who are financially embarrassed and unable to pay him until next month, £100.

Stock of fruit and vegetables at end of period at market value £1,500.

Payments made during period:

	£
Vehicle running expenses	100
Vehicle licence—annual	130
Rent paid	60
Weekend help	60
Payments made to creditors for supplies	2,000

What is his profit for the period? What is the financial position at the end of the period? Does this represent accurately the worth of his business?

INCOME STATEMENT ANSWERS
Tom Smith—Barrow boy

3.1

Income statement
for the first four weeks

	£	£
Sales		2,485
Cost of goods sold:		
Opening stock	—	
Add Purchases	1,500	
	1,500	
Less Closing stock	50	1,450
Gross profit		1,035
Expenses:		
Rent	60	
Weekend help	60	
Fines	80	
Depreciation:		
Barrow	32	
Scales	4	236
NET PROFIT		799

Cash statement

	£	£
Opening balance		3,000
Add Receipts		2,485
Cash available		5,485
Deduct Payments:		
Rent	45	
Weekend help	60	
Fines	80	
Fruit	1,500	
Barrow	832	
Scales	208	2,725
CASH IN HAND		2,760

Balance sheet
as at end of first four weeks

	Cost £	Depreciation £	Net book value (NBV) £		£
Fixed assets:				Capital	3,000
Scales	208	4	204	RESERVES	
Barrow	832	32	800	Profit	799
	1,040	36	1,004		
Current assets:				Current liabilities:	
Stock		50		Rent due	15
Bank		2,760	2,810		
			3,814		3,814

The depreciation is calculated as follows:

The barrow cost £832 and is expected to last for two years. Tom Smith prepares his accounts every four weeks, and as there are 52 weeks in a year he has 52/4 = 13 accounting periods. In two years he will have 26 accounting periods. The barrow does not have any scrap value so the depreciation is 832/26 = £32.

Similarly the depreciation of the scales is over four years which is 4 × 13 = 52 periods. The calculation is 208/52 = £4.

Depreciation does not appear in the cash statement because it allocates the cost of the assets but does not cause any more money to leave Smith's business.

The sales figure is calculated by adding to the takings the expenses that have been paid out of them: £2,300 + £185 = £2,485.

The barrow and scales do not have a direct impact on the income statement because as far as Smith is concerned they are fixed assets.

The closing stock has been valued at the lower of cost or current market value.

3.2

Income statement
for the second four weeks

	£	£
Sales		2,800
Cost of goods sold:		
Opening stock	50	
Add Purchases	2,000	
	2,050	
Less Closing stock	100	1,950
Gross profit		850
Expenses:		
Rent	60	
Weekend help	60	
Fines	150	
Insurance	8	
Depreciation:		
Barrow	32	
Scales	4	314
NET PROFIT		536

Cash statement

	£	£
Opening balance		2,760
Add Receipts		2,800
Cash available		5,560
Deduct Payments:		
Insurance	104	
Wife	200	
Rent	45	
Fines	150	
Weekend help	60	
Fruit	2,000	2,559
CASH IN HAND		3,001

Balance sheet
as at end of second four weeks

	Cost £	Depreciation £	NBV £		£	£
Fixed assets:				Capital		3,000
Scales	208	8	200	RESERVES		
Barrow	832	64	768	Profit b/fwd	799	
	1,040	72	968			
				Add This period	536	
					1,335	
				Less Drawings	200	1,135
Current assets:				Current liabilities:		
Stock		100		Rent due		30
Bank		3,001				
Insurance prepaid		96	3,197			
			4,165			4,165

The profit for the second period is £536. His cash balance at the end of the second period is £3,001. His financial position as reflected in the balance sheet is sound but he does seem to have rather too much money lying idle.

He has made a profit of £536 and has a great deal of cash, so he could afford to give his wife £400. It is good policy to retain some profit in the business to allow it to expand, so Smith should not give his wife much more than £400 as he would be approaching the total profit figure.

3.3

Income statement
for the third four weeks

	£	£
Sales		3,300
Cost of goods sold:		
Opening stock	100	
Add Purchases	2,500	
	2,600	
Less Closing stock	200	2,400
Gross profit		900
Expenses:		
Rent	60	
Weekend help	60	
Fines	25	
Insurance	8	
Depreciation:		
Barrow	32	
Scales	4	189
Operating profit		711
Loss on sale of barrow		236
NET PROFIT		475

Cash statement

	£	£
Opening balance		3,001
Add Receipts		3,800
Cash available		6,801
Deduct payments:		
Wife	450	
Rent	75	
Weekend help	60	
Fruit	2,500	
Van	3,003	6,088
CASH IN HAND		713

Balance sheet
as at end of third four weeks

	Cost	Depre-ciation	NBV			£	£
	£	£	£				
Fixed assets:				Capital			3,000
Scales	208	12	196	RESERVES			
Van	3,003	—	3,003	Profit b/fwd		1,135	
				Add This period		475	
	3,211	12	3,199				
						1,610	
				Less Drawings		450	1,160
Current assets:				Current liabilities:			
Stock		200		Rent due		15	
Insurance prepaid		88		Fine pending		25	40
Bank		713	1,001				
			4,200				4,200

The loss on the sale of the barrow is calculated as follows:

Cost of barrow		832
Less Depreciation (£32 × 3)		96
Book value at time of sale		736
Deduct Proceeds of sale		500
Loss on sale		£236

The operating profit of £711 is the profit from normal business activities. The net profit of £475 is arrived at only after extraordinary items, like the sale of the barrow, have been taken into account.

The accounting convention of anticipating losses has been taken into account in providing £25 for the anticipated fine.

The barrow has a full period's depreciation as it was sold on the last day of the period. The van is not depreciated at all as it was obtained on the last day of the period.

Smith has made a loss on the sale of his barrow of £236; his operating profit for the period is £711 and his financial position at the end of the period as revealed by the balance sheet is sound. It is interesting to note that his cash balance has fallen, mainly due to the purchase of the van.

3.4

Income statement
for the fourth four weeks

	£	£
Sales		3,600
Cost of goods sold:		
Opening stock	200	
Add Purchases	4,000	
	4,200	
Less Closing stock	1,500	2,700
Gross profit		900
Overprovision for fine recovered		5
		905
Expenses:		
Vehicle running	100	
Rent	60	
Weekend help	60	
Insurance	8	
Vehicle licence	10	
Depreciation:		
Scales	4	
Van	85	327
NET PROFIT		578

Cash statement

	£	£
Opening balance		713
Add Receipts		3,500
Cash available		4,213
Deduct payments:		
Wife	500	
Rent	60	
Weekend help	60	
Fruit	3,500	
Fine	20	
Vehicle running	100	
Licence	130	4,370
BANK OVERDRAWN		(157)

Balance sheet
as at end of fourth four weeks

	Cost	Depre- ciation	NBV			
	£	£	£		£	£
Fixed assets:				Capital		3,000
Scales	208	16	192	RESERVES		
Van	3,003	85	2,918	Profit b/fwd	1,160	
	3,211	101	3,110	*Add* This period	578	
					1,738	
				Less Drawings	500	1,238
Current assets:				Current liabilities:		
Stock		1,500		Creditor	500	
Debtor		100		Rent due	15	
Insurance prepaid		80		Bank overdraft	157	672
Licence prepaid		120	1,800			
			4,910			4,910

The depreciation of the van is calculated as follows:

$$\text{Depreciation} = \frac{\text{Cost} - \text{Scrap value}}{\text{Life}} = \frac{3{,}003 - 793}{26} = \frac{2110}{26} = £85$$

The overprovision for the fine of £5 is treated as an additional receipt. This is because the last period's profit was reduced by £5, and to compensate for that this period's profit is increased by £5.

The vehicle licence is treated as capital expenditure. Only one-thirteenth of it is used up in this period and shown in the income statement as an expense. The balance is shown on the balance sheet as an asset.

Despite being profitable Smith has a bank overdraft of £157, and it is essential for him to convince his wife that she can manage on £400 per month, or less, if he is to survive in the short term.

In the longer term it may be that his business will pick up and his situation improve as he begins to gain a better understanding of his new situation.

Smith's net profit for the period is £578. Smith's financial position at the end of the period is somewhat precarious as previously stated. If he can learn from his experience and obtain his wife's cooperation, he should overcome this problem, with the aid of the bank. It might be prudent for him to obtain overdraft facilities of £2,000 and prepare a cash flow forecast.

His balance sheet does not accurately represent the worth of his business as assets are valued on the basis of historical cost, less depreciation, and no account has been taken of goodwill, which would be whatever he would persuade a purchaser to give him for his business as a going concern.

FOUR

CASH BUDGET (CASH FLOW FORECAST)

We have seen in the previous chapter that profitability does not mean liquidity and that many profitable firms fail through lack of liquidity. In order to reduce the likelihood of this happening a cash flow forecast or budget should be prepared annually and carefully monitored, if possible on a weekly basis, but certainly once a month.

A cash budget is a forecast of future cash requirements that is prepared one year in advance, broken down into monthly figures to show the anticipated surplus or deficit at the start of the month, plus cash receipts in the month less cash payments in the month, which will give the anticipated cash in hand at the end of the month. Collecting the figures to put into the cash budget is, however, rather more difficult, because to forecast accurately your activities for a year ahead is virtually impossible, but with a little practice forecasts can be made accurate enough to make them well worth while.

It is very important to monitor your forecast for each month during the year, then, if for some reason your forecast is wrong, you have the opportunity to take action to improve the cash situation before it becomes critical. This is an extremely useful tool in managing a business and many fail because they do not plan their cash needs. It will greatly increase your chances of success if you go to your bank manager with a well-prepared cash budget to ask for a loan or overdraft six months before you need the money, rather than waiting until the need has arisen and then wondering what to do about it. If you are aware of the situation far enough in advance, it may be possible to amend your plans and so avoid the cash deficit altogether.

A cash budget has been drawn up as an example of one of the ways in which it can be done. It is not the only way and you may prefer some other approach. The starting point is the cash position as it stands now and the rest of the information is inserted on your best estimate of the likely happenings of the next year. You may need more or less detailed descriptions of the items according to your requirements.

Example   *Cash budget for six months, January to June*

	Jan £'000s	Feb £'000s	Mar £'000s	April £'000s	May £'000s	June £'000s
Opening cash balance overdrawn	(11)	—	—	—	(38)	(13)
Opening cash balance in hand	—	17	53	60	—	—
Receipts:			74		75	
Cash receipts from cash sales	70	75	96	80	95	80
Cash receipts from credit sales	90	100	—	100	—	100
Miscellaneous cash receipts	—	5		—		—
TOTAL CASH AVAILABLE	149	197	223	240	132	167
Payments:						
Payment for wages	50	55	54	60	56	60
Cash purchases	20	20	22	25	24	25
Payments for previous credit purchases	60	65	64	65	60	64
Loan interest	—	—	20	—	—	—
Loan repaid	—	—	—	—	—	—
Rent paid	—	—	—	5	—	—
Rates paid	—	—	—	10	—	—
Electricity paid	—	—	—	5	—	—
Gas paid	—	—	—	3	—	—
Postage paid	1	2	1	3	2	2
Telephone paid	—	—	—	—	1	—
Miscellaneous	1	2	2	2	2	2
Capital payments	—	—	—	100	—	—
TOTAL PAYMENTS	132	144	163	278	145	153
TOTAL CASH − TOTAL PAYMENTS ( ) = deficit	17	53	60	(38)	(13)	14

Thus £14,000 opening cash balance in hand would be carried forward for July.

In the example given April has a cash deficit of £38,000 shown by writing the figure in brackets, thus (£38,000). The owner of the business would have been aware of this some time before it occurred and, through preparing his cash budget and monitoring it regularly, would have been able to take the action necessary to overcome a potentially critical cash shortage. A suggested form for the preparation of a cash budget is given overleaf. Other styles may be used if preferred as the important thing is the preparation of the cash budget and not the form it takes.

In preparing the cash budget the opening balance would be known but all the other figures would be uncertain to a greater or lesser extent. The estimates would be prepared on the basis of the figures for the previous period adjusted for any changes that you think may take place. For example, if you anticipate a wage increase of 10 per cent as from April then you would increase your salary estimate accordingly. The same sort of approach is needed for all your estimates and, with experience, your forecasts will become more accurate.

Note The cash budget as the name implies refers only to **cash** and excludes non-cash items, like depreciation, which affect only profit.

Answer the cash flow forecast questions below on the blank table. Compare your answer with the suggested one.

Suggested form of cash budget for six months, July to December

	July £	Aug £	Sept £	Oct £	Nov £	Dec £
Opening balance						
Sales receipts						
Legacy						
TOTAL CASH AVAILABLE						
Payments:						
Labour						
Materials						
Variable expenses						
Fixed expenses						
Capital expenditure						
TOTAL PAYMENTS						
TOTAL CASH – TOTAL PAYMENTS						
Balance carried f/wd						

CASH FLOW FORECAST QUESTION

4.1 Draw up the cash budget for D. Davies from the following information for the six months for 1 July to 31 December 19--:

1. Opening cash balance at 1 July 19-- is £1,500.
2. Sales at £20 per unit (figures in units):

April	May	June	July	Aug	Sept	Oct	Nov	Dec
110	120	140	160	180	190	130	80	70

Debtors will pay two months after they have bought the goods.
3. £5 per unit direct labour is payable in the same month as production.
4. Raw materials cost £6 per unit and are paid for three months after the goods are used in production.

5. Production in units:

April	May	June	July	Aug	Sept	Oct	Nov	Dec	Jan
150	170	180	200	130	110	100	90	70	60

6. Other variable expenses are £3 per unit. Two-thirds of this cost is paid for in the same month as production and one-third in the month following production.
7. Fixed expenses of £150 per month are paid one month in arrears.
8. Capital expenditure for September is £6,000.
9. Davies expects a legacy of £3,000 in December and will pay it into the business bank account.

ANSWER
4.1

	July £	Aug £	Sept £	Oct £	Nov £	Dec £
Opening balance	1,500	1,270	1,790	(3,140)	(1,700)	440
Sales receipts	2,400	2,800	3,200	3,600	3,800	2,600
Legacy	—	—	—	—	—	3,000
TOTAL CASH AVAILABLE	3,900	4,070	4,990	460	2,100	6,040
Payments:						
Labour	1,000	650	550	500	450	350
Materials	900	1,020	1,080	1,200	780	660
Variable expenses	{ 180	{ 200	{ 130	{ 110	{ 100	{ 90
	400	260	220	200	180	140
Fixed expenses	150	150	150	150	150	150
Capital expenditure	—	—	6,000	—	—	—
TOTAL PAYMENTS	2,630	2,280	8,130	2,160	1,660	1,390
TOTAL CASH — TOTAL PAYMENTS						
Balance carried f/wd	1,270	1,790	(3,140)	(1,700)	440	4,650

You can see that there is a cash crisis in September and October. If the owner of the business had been monitoring his forecast he would have been aware of this up to 12 months before it occurred. This would have given him the opportunity to obtain bank overdraft facilities in good time or perhaps to have rescheduled his capital outlay. If he could delay this for three months the amount of overdraft that he requires would be nil.

FIVE

INTERPRETATION

The final accounts of companies contain many indications of their financial health. This information is of value to shareholders and creditors as well as to the management of the company. The data contained in the accounts may be interpreted by means of ratio analysis, which defines meaningful relationships between business results. Examples are profit on sales and return on capital employed. There are four broad categories of ratios that are useful in assessing a company's performance and financial position. These are:

1. Profitability ratios
2. Short-term liquidity ratio
3. Long-term solvency ratios
4. Efficiency ratios

It is important to realize that with financial ratios the figures alone have very little meaning. They have to be compared with something, i.e.,

1. The figures for the previous four years, say, so that a trend may be seen
2. Figures for similar firms in the same industry (shown in the annually published Industrial Performance Analysis)
3. Where possible, the industry average
4. With the business plan

These ratios are further explored using the example of a manufacturing concern shown on pages 38 to 40.

Manufacturing Business Ltd
Income statement
(manufacturing, trading and profit and loss account)
for the year ending 30 November 19--

	£	£
Cost of material used:		
Opening stock of raw materials	20,000	
Add Purchases of raw materials	70,000	
	90,000	
Deduct Closing stock of raw materials	40,000	
Raw materials used		50,000
Manufacturing labour		20,000
Prime or direct cost of goods made:		70,000
Indirect manufacturing costs:		
Labour (supervisors and cleaning staff)	5,000	
Heat and light of factory or workshop	2,000	
Rent and rates of factory or workshop	10,000	
Depreciation of factory/workshop equipment and machinery	8,000	
General manufacturing expenses	3,000	28,000
		98,000
Add Opening work in progress (WIP)		3,000
		101,000
Deduct Closing work in progress (WIP)		1,000
Factory cost of goods made transferred:		100,000

	£	£
Sales		180,000
Cost of sales (cost of goods sold):		
Opening stock of finished goods	5,000	
Add Factory cost of goods made transferred	100,000	
	105,000	
Deduct Closing stock of finished goods	45,000	
Cost of sales		60,000
Gross profit		120,000
Administrative and selling expenses:		
Wages	8,000	
Advertising	1,000	
Rates	2,000	
Light and heat	500	
General expenses	500	
Depreciation	1,200	
Bank charges	200	13,400
NET PROFIT BEFORE TAX		106,600

Corporation tax } These entries depend on the rate of corporation tax and the
Net profit after tax } necessary adjustments.

Manufacturing Business Ltd
Balance sheet as at 30 November 19--

	Cost £	Depreciation £	Net book value (NBV) £
Fixed assets:			
Land and buildings	800,000	100,000	700,000
Plant and machinery	400,000	60,000	340,000
Fixtures and fittings	100,000	30,000	70,000
Motor vehicles	10,000	6,000	4,000
	1,310,000	196,000	1,114,000
Current assets:			
Stock			
Raw materials	40,000		
WIP	1,000		
Finished goods	45,000		
	86,000		
Debtors	4,000		
Bank	2,000		
Cash	500		
		92,500	
Deduct Current liabilities:			
Dividend due	5,000		
Creditors	41,500		
		46,500	
Working capital			46,000
NET CAPITAL EMPLOYED			1,160,000
Financed by:			
Authorized and issued share capital:			
900,000 £1 ordinary shares		900,000	
200,000 10 per cent preference shares		200,000	
		1,100,000	
Reserves:			
General	40,000		
Profit and loss account	20,000	60,000	
			1,160,000

5.1 PROFITABILITY RATIOS

Most businesses exist primarily to earn profits for their owners, which makes the ratio of profit to capital extremely important. This is so much the case that the expression:

$$\frac{\text{Profit}}{\text{Capital}}$$

is often called the 'primary ratio'.

Unfortunately, profit and capital can be calculated in different ways, which makes comparison of the profitability of different businesses somewhat suspect. However, it is a good guide to general performance.

Profit to net capital employed

Net capital employed is equal to the total assets of a business minus its current liabilities.

1. *Gross profit to net capital employed.* This ratio is useful as a means of control. The gross profit to net capital employed should not vary significantly from one accounting year to another. If it does vary management should be aware of the causes of the fluctuation. The ratio in our example is:

$$\frac{\text{Gross profit} \times 100}{\text{Net capital employed}} = \frac{120,000 \times 100}{1,160,000} = 10.34 \text{ per cent}$$

2. *Net profit before tax to net capital employed* (also called *Return on Capital Employed*—ROCE). This ratio indicates the performance of the net assets of the company. It is an overall indicator of management performance and includes the effect of both operating efficiencies and financial efficiencies. The ratio in isolation is not very meaningful. It should be compared with the return that would be obtained from investing in the Post Office savings or building societies or in the banks. This will indicate whether or not you would be wise to discontinue your business, invest the proceeds and work for somebody else. The decision is never as clear-cut as that since many people prefer to work for themselves no matter how low the return on their investment. Trends over several years will show whether the result obtained is unusual or as expected for that business. Comparison with the industry average will show whether you are doing better or worse than the others. The ratio in our example is:

$$\frac{\text{Net profit before tax} \times 100}{\text{Net capital employed}} = \frac{106,600 \times 100}{1,160,000} = 9.19 \text{ per cent}$$

How does this compare with the return from the Post Office, bank, building society or the average figure for the sector in which your organization operates?

Profit on sales

This ratio expresses the gross profitability as a percentage of sales. Gross profit to sales must be healthy if the business is to survive. The figure on its own means little and it should be compared with that for the previous four years and with the average for the industry.

This will enable you to say whether or not it is an unusual result and also if you are doing better than the industry average. The ratio in our example is:

$$\frac{\text{Gross profit} \times 100}{\text{Net sales}} = \frac{120{,}000 \times 100}{180{,}000} = 66.67 \text{ per cent}$$

This seems a reasonable return but without the additional information mentioned above we are not able to comment. However, it does provide sufficient for the expenses to be met without using all the profit for the year.

5.2 SHORT-TERM LIQUIDITY RATIOS

Approximately 80 per cent of the companies that fail in the UK are profitable at the time that they do so. Lack of money with which to pay their way forces them into liquidation. The importance of the liquidity ratios lies in the fact that they can help to avoid this situation.

Current ratio

This is a measure of an organization's ability to pay its way in the medium term, that is, from about four to nine months in the future. The current ratio expresses the current assets as a ratio of the current liabilities. The ratio in our example is:

Current assets:Current liabilities
92,500   :46,500
1.99   :1

This is not meaningful in isolation. The trend over the last four years might show that it has suddenly dropped from 5:1 to 1.99:1 in which case it would warrant further investigation. On the other hand it might have been 1.97:1 for the previous years in which case there would probably be no need for further investigation. The ratios should always be read in conjunction with the available balance sheet information. In this case it does appear that there might be a liquidity problem since £86,000 of the current assets are tied up in stock. Various ratios are stated as giving the required margin of safety for a company and 2:1 is often quoted as the minimum to allow for safe operation. This is nonsense, for if we look at the 1990 published accounts of three companies that do not seem to have any liquidity problems, i.e., Marks and Spencer plc, J. Sainsbury plc, Tesco plc, we will see that their current ratios are:

	Marks and Spencer plc	J. Sainsbury plc	Tesco plc
	£	£	£
Current assets	907,300,000	599,300,000	275,400,000
Current liabilities	912,500,000	1,352,300,000	749,400,000
Current assets : Current liabilities	0.99 : 1	0.44 : 1	0.37 : 1

I do not believe anyone would claim that any of these three companies was about to go out of business due to a liquidity shortage. You should remember, however, that this *does not mean* that all companies could operate on these ratios. What it does emphasize is the fact that different industries work on and need different working capital.

The figures for Rolls Royce plc and Ward Holdings plc in their 1990 accounts are:

	Rolls Royce plc £	*Ward Holdings plc* £
Current assets	1,951,000,000	72,986,000
Current liabilities	841,000,000	12,780,000
Current assets : Current liabilities	2.3 : 1	5.7 : 1

A more sensitive ratio which will give us a better idea of whether or not the company has liquidity problems is shown below.

Quick ratio (acid test)

This is a measure of an organization's ability to pay its way in the short term, that is up to about four months in the future. It expresses the quick assets as a ratio of the current liabilities, that is, those assets which may readily be turned into cash, together with the cash and bank figures. The ratio is our example in:

Quick assets:Current liabilities
6,500   :46,500
0.14   :1

This is not meaningful in isolation although it does seem rather low. The trend for the last four years will show whether it is unusually low as will the average for the industry. If we study the balance sheet it shows that we have creditors of £41,500 and debtors, bank and cash balances of only £6,500. This does indicate a quite serious liquidity problem and steps should be taken to alleviate it. It would be possible to raise a loan secured on the premises for £100,000, which would dramatically improve the liquidity of the company, or the bank may be prepared to provide overdraft facilities if it was convinced that the profitability of the company could be maintained or improved. The quoted safe ratio for the acid test is 1:1 but this again is rubbish. There is no ideal ratio since what is good for one business is bad for another. If we look at our five companies again we see:

	Marks and Spencer plc £	*J. Sainsbury plc* £	*Tesco plc* £
Quick assets	533,000,000	290,900,000	62,600,000
Current liabilities	912,500,000	1,352,300,000	749,400,000
Quick assets : current liabilities	0.58 : 1	0.22 : 1	0.08 : 1

	Rolls Royce plc £	*Ward Holdings plc* £
Quick assets	1,250,000,000	3,284,000
Current liabilities	841,000,000	12,780,000
Quick assets : Current liabilities	1.5 : 1	0.26 : 1

Four of these companies are running successfully on ratios of less than 1:1, other companies need ratios of over 1:1 depending on their industrial sector and methods of operation. Sainsbury and Tesco can operate on such low ratios because the bulk of their sales are for cash. In using these ratios it should be remembered that it is as bad to be too liquid as it is to have too little liquidity. There may be some concern over Ward Holdings, which is a building company, in that it may need to generate more liquidity by selling some assets in order to pay its way.

5.3 LONG-TERM SOLVENCY RATIOS

Businesses can obtain the funds that they require by issuing shares, both ordinary and preference. The ordinary shareholders have the equity of the business and become the owners. Money can be borrowed by means of debentures, or bank overdraft facilities may be obtained. However the funds are obtained, there is a rule that it is wise to follow if you wish to avoid problems in the future. The rule is that you do not borrow short to invest long. The fringe banks ignored this rule in 1972 and some of them went out of existence, others were saved by larger banks. So far as the business in our example, or any other business is concerned, it means that the fixed assets should be bought out of long-term capital, that is equity, i.e., the owner's interest, or debentures. In our example we have fixed assets of £1,114,000 and share capital and reserves, i.e., equity interest, of £1,160,000 and so we are following the rule. Had we not done so we would have added an additional strain to the working capital.

Too much borrowing causes dramatic changes in the return to ordinary shareholders when profits fluctuate only slightly and puts the company at risk. Companies that have a high proportion of fixed interest loan capital to equity are said to be highly geared, and these companies may find that they cannot survive at all if profits fall or exchange rates alter. A recent example of this was Polly Peck which was extremely highly geared. The following illustrates the effect of gearing on profit available to ordinary shareholders:

	A Co. £	B Co. £
Capital structure		
Ordinary share capital £1 shares	1,000,000	250,000
Retained profits	500,000	500,000
Equity interest (due to ordinary shareholders)	1,500,000	750,000
10 per cent Debenture loan	250,000	1,000,000
	1,750,000	1,750,000
	Low gearing	High gearing

Let us suppose that profits before interest and tax earned by the two companies are exactly the same and they fluctuate between £100,000 and £400,000, then the impact on the ordinary shareholder may be traced as being:

	A Co.			B Co.		
	£'000s	£'000s	£'000s	£'000s	£'000s	£'000s
Profit before interest	100	200	400	100	200	400
Debenture interest	25	25	25	100	100	100
Profit after interest	75	175	375	0	100	300
Tax 52 per cent	39	91	195	0	52	156
Profit available to shareholders	36	84	180	0	48	144
Earnings per share	4p	8p	18p	0p	19p	58p

The earnings per share are calculated by dividing the available profit by the number of shares.

$$\text{For A Co. the first calculation is } \frac{36,000}{1,000,000} = £0.04$$

$$\text{For B Co. the second calculation is } \frac{48,000}{250,000} = £0.19$$

This clearly illustrates the fact that if profits are rising it is better to buy shares in a highly geared company and if they are falling you would be wise to be with a company that has low gearing. The earnings per share fluctuate greatly with profits in Company B, ranging from 0 to 58p, whereas in Company A they only fluctuate between 4p and 18p.

Capital gearing ratio

$$\frac{\text{Equity capital}}{\text{Fixed investment borrowing}}$$

There is no accepted relationship but you should remember the risk of high gearing (sometimes called leverage). In our example we have a ratio of infinity since we have no borrowing at all. It may be that the organization should seriously consider some borrowing to improve its liquidity, and, if the resources are properly employed, it should be possible to increase the earnings per share.

The practice of 'off balance sheet financing' has made it extremely difficult to assess how highly geared companies are simply by looking at the balance sheet. Concern has been increased by the collapse of Polly Peck amongst others, and the problems of organizations like Brent Walker, because lack of information in the balance sheet make it impossible for analysts to foresee the problems. Things have now reached such a state that many people are querying the value of income statements and balance sheets in their current form and demanding a complete revision of the way in which they are presented and the information that they contain.

Off balance sheet financing

This is the practice of showing what is often a liability of an organization in the balance sheet as an asset. It is not done intentionally in order to mislead would-be investors or suppliers but it is becoming a rather frequent occurrence. A company's balance sheet may show:

	£'000s	£'000s
Fixed assets:		
Land and buildings		900
Plant and machinery		60
Motor vehicles		10
Investment in subsidiary undertakings		80
		1050
Current assets		
Stocks	40	
Debtors	80	
Bank	10	
	130	
Less current liabilities	110	
WORKING CAPITAL		20
NET CAPITAL EMPLOYED		1070
Financed by:		
Issued share capital		
4,000,000 ordinary shares		1000
Reserves		
Profit and loss account		20
Long-term loan		50
		1070

This company would seem low geared and safe to deal with. What would not be revealed in the balance sheet is that the subsidiary company, for which it is responsible, is extremely highly geared with borrowings of £900,000. If this were shown it would present a very different picture indeed. You can see from this why balance sheets often have to be treated with utmost caution and further enquiries undertaken before any major decision is made.

Times interest earned

$$\frac{\text{Profit before fixed interest charges}}{\text{Fixed interest charges}}$$

This indicates the safety margin to allow the company to survive. If interest charges are equal to or greater than the earnings, then the company will not survive for long and there will be no surplus for shareholders/owners. The calculation is not relevant to our example since we have no borrowing. This ratio and the previous one may, however, be illustrated using the example of A Company and B Company.

Capital gearing ratio

	A Co.	B Co.
$\dfrac{\text{Equity capital}}{\text{Fixed investment borrowing}} =$	$\dfrac{1,500,000}{250,000}$	$\dfrac{750,000}{1,000,000}$
	1:6	1:0.75

Times interest earned Using the middle case for both companies we have:

$\dfrac{\text{Profit before fixed interest charges}}{\text{Fixed interest charges}} =$	$\dfrac{200,000}{25,000}$	$\dfrac{200,000}{100,000}$
	8 times	2 times

5.4 EFFICIENCY RATIOS

It is essential for anyone running a business to know how efficiently he is doing so. The following three ratios will enable you to keep an eye on the business without becoming too immersed in details:

Debtors' ratio

$$\frac{\text{Debtors}}{\text{Average daily credit sales}}$$

This measures the average time to collect a debt and when more companies are failing daily because they cannot pay their way, it is an extremely important ratio. No business can survive today if it is failing to collect sums of money that are due to it within a reasonable period of time. In the Manufacturing Business example, if we assume that none of the sales are for cash and they have taken place evenly throughout the working year of, say, 360 days, then the daily average is:

$$\frac{£180,000}{360} = £500$$

The debtors from the balance sheet are £4,000 which represents:

$$\frac{4,000}{500} = 8 \text{ days' sales}$$

The company is taking approximately one week to collect moneys due to it, which is exceptionally good. Had the answer been four months, then there would have been cause for concern and action would have had to be taken to remedy the situation.

Creditors' ratio

$$\frac{\text{Creditors}}{\text{Average daily credit purchases}}$$

This measures the average time taken to pay a debt. The answer in the present climate is to keep your supplier waiting as long as you decently can without impairing the relationship that you have built up with him. In our example, if we assume that all purchases are on credit and that they have taken place evenly throughout the year of 360 days, then the daily average is:

$$\frac{70,000}{360} = £194.44$$

The creditors from the balance sheet are £41,500 which represents:

$$\frac{41,500}{194.44} = 213 \text{ days' sales}$$

The business is taking 30 weeks to pay its suppliers. This is far too long and may be a reflection of the liquidity problem that it has. Steps should be taken to correct the situation before suppliers lose confidence and refuse any further credit. Had payment been made in 14 days that would have been too short a period and more credit could have been safely taken.

Stock turnover

$$\frac{\text{Cost of goods sold}}{\text{Average stock of finished goods}}$$

This helps to ensure that you do not tie up large volumes of working capital in stocks. Within reason the faster you turn over your stock the better, as long as you avoid running round in circles and getting nowhere. This can help ensure that your stock does not increase without your being aware of it. In our example cost of goods sold is £60,000 and a rough average stock can be obtained from:

$$\frac{\text{Opening stock} + \text{Closing stock}}{2} = \frac{5,000 + 45,000}{2} = £25,000$$

so the calculation becomes:

$$\frac{\text{Cost of goods sold}}{\text{Average stock of finished goods}} = \frac{60,000}{25,000} = 2.4 \text{ times per year}$$

To convert this to days you simply divide it into the number of sales days in the year. The figure usually taken for sales days is 360 and so we have:

$$\frac{360}{2.4} = 150 \text{ days}$$

The stock being turned over in 150 days. This ratio in isolation is not very meaningful and should be compared with the last three to four years' figures as well as the industry average. Stocks naturally increase as sales expand, or there would be nothing left to sell, and contract as sales fall. For companies like wholesalers and some retailers a high turnover is essential if any profit is to be made at all. Obsolete stock lying in store would cause a low rate of stock turnover and should be immediately dealt with.

Mark-up

$$\frac{(\text{Selling price} - \text{Cost price}) \times 100}{\text{Cost price}}$$

This tells the owner or manager how much is being added to the cost price of the goods to arrive at the selling price. Having decided how much should be added it is important that it is maintained from period to period. If the mark-up is reduced profitability will suffer unless turnover can be increased sufficiently or fixed costs reduced. No change in mark-up should occur without you being fully aware of it.

In our example the cost of goods sold is £60,000 and the selling price is £180,000, so the mark-up is

$$\frac{(£180,000 - £60,000) \times 100}{£60,000} = \frac{£120,000 \times 100}{£60,000} = 200\%$$

Two hundred per cent is being added to the cost price of the goods to arrive at the selling price. The management has decided that this is sufficient to meet all the fixed costs and leave a reasonable profit. The figure is not very meaningful in isolation but it is extremely helpful for control purposes when comparing one month or year with another.

There are a great many ratios that it is possible to use to help you control your business. Those mentioned above are some of the more useful but it should be remembered that in themselves they produce no answers. However, they do ask some relevant questions, and, when used in conjunction with other information, provide indicators that if properly used can help your business to avoid many pitfalls and may even prevent it going into liquidation.

INTERPRETATION QUESTION

5.1 On the following page are the summarized balance sheets of Polytam plc on 31 December 1990 and 31 December 1991. Polytam is in the engineering field.

	1990 £'000s	1991 £'000s		1990 £'000s	1991 £'000s
Freehold property at valuation 31.12.90	180	180	Authorized and issued share capital	300	300
Equipment (cost less depreciation)	170	130	Fixed asset re-valuation reserve	80	80
Investment at cost	50	—	Income statement balance	70	85
				450	465
Current assets					
Stocks:			15% debenture loan		
Materials	90	60	redeemable 1996–97	180	180
Work in progress and finished goods	100	95	Current liabilities:		
(Uncompleted long-term contracts)	300	250	Creditors	300	240
			Bank overdraft	190	200
Debtors	230	370			
	1,120	1,085		1,120	1,085

The following are the summarized income statements for the years ending 31 December 1990 and 31 December 1991.

	1990 £'000s	1990 £'000s	1991 £'000s	1991 £'000s
Sales		1,700		1,300
Gain on sale of investment		—		60
Gain arising from change in basis of accounting for long-term contracts		—		190
		1,700		1,550
Deduct:				
Salaries and wages	420		380	
Materials	870		790	
General expenses	300	1,590	280	1,450
NET PROFIT		110		100

In the 1990 balance sheet contracts were shown at cost. The long-term contracts in the 1991 accounts include anticipated profit attributable to the work undertaken on them up to the date of the balance sheet.

The company has overdraft facilities of £210,000 secured by a floating charge on its assets. The facilities are fully utilized on 23 March 1992 and the managing director is considering what to do. He considers the accounts for 1991 and sends out the following note stating what he feels has happened:

> The year to December 1991 was bad. We suffered from the full weight of the recession. Our total sales fell with inevitable consequences for our trading results. The situation was made worse by staff changes in our accounting department where control has slipped. We have now engaged a first class man to get this side sorted out.
>   There are obvious problems which have caused a temporary set-back but we are now overcoming them and have every confidence in producing good results this year.

Fully discuss the financial position of Polytam plc using any ratios that you feel would be helpful.

ANSWER
5.1

	1990	*1991*

1. Net profit as a percentage of net capital employed $\dfrac{110 \times 100}{630} = 17.46$ per cent

$$\dfrac{100 \times 100}{645} = \qquad\qquad 15.5 \text{ per cent}$$

In 1991 if the extraordinary items are excluded there is a loss of £150,000 viz.,

Gain on sale of investment   60,000
Gain on change in accounting basis   190,000
                                      ―――――――
                                       250,000

This indicates the extent of the collapse in operating viability on a consistent basis with the 1990 accounts.

2. Sales/Debtors ratio (£'000s) $= \dfrac{\text{Debtors}}{\text{Average daily credit sales}}$

$\dfrac{\text{Sales}}{360} = \dfrac{1,700}{360} = £4.72 = \dfrac{230}{4.72} = \qquad 49 \text{ days}$

$\dfrac{\text{Sales}}{360} = \dfrac{1,300}{360} = £3.61 = \dfrac{370}{3.61} = \qquad 103 \text{ days}$

This shows that debt collection has slipped dramatically and is in keeping with the reported problems in the accounting department.

3. *Current ratio*
   Current assets:Current liabilities
   720:490   1.47:1
   775:440   1.76:1
4. *Quick ratio*
   Quick assets:Current liabilities
   530:490   1.08:1
   620:440   1.41:1

The improvement in these ratios has been brought about by the change in accounting basis.

5. *Creditors' ratio*

This can be calculated only roughly as we do not know what the purchase figure for materials is. However, by substituting materials used for purchases we have creditors to average daily materials used.

If we assume there are 360 days in the year

then daily use is $\dfrac{870}{360} = 2.42$ *1990*   *1991*

and $\dfrac{790}{360} = 2.19$

then the ratio becomes $\dfrac{300}{2.42} =$ 124 days

and $\dfrac{240}{2.19} =$ 110 days

The suppliers are giving approximately 16 weeks' credit which is exceptional and implies special terms. The reliance on credit questions the relationship with suppliers.

There is no evidence that the company has turned the corner and although it is perfectly proper for an organization to change the basis of its accounting, comparisons must be made of like with like. There is no support for the managing director's confidence that 1992 will show an improvement although completion of contracts and better debt collection could bring this about.

FUNDS FLOW

Criticism is often made of the published accounts of companies in that they show that profit has been made or loss incurred but not what has happened to it. Many managers feel that the profit should be reflected in an increased bank balance or reduced overdraft and are perplexed when this does not prove to be the case. Companies have noted this and now include in their published accounts a funds flow statement, or sources and applications of funds statement. This not only shows what funds have been generated by the undertaking in the period under review but also whether a surplus or deficit has been made.

In order to prepare a funds flow statement you need the balance sheet at the start of the period under review and the balance sheet at the end of the period so that the two can be compared and changes noted; and the profit and depreciation for the period which will be found in the income statement. The rules that are followed in the preparation of the funds flow statements when comparing the two balance sheets are:

Sources of funds
Increase in liabilities
Decreases in assets at cost (exclude depreciation which does not affect funds)
Uses of funds
Decrease in liabilities
Increase in assets

Profit is also a source of funds so long as it is retained in the organization, and loss is a use of funds. An example will help to illustrate this concept.

Micro
Balance sheet as at 30 June

	1990 £'000s	1991 £'000s		1990 £'000s	1991 £'000s
Fixed assets:					
Land and buildings at cost	800	850	Ordinary shares	600	850
Plant and machinery at cost	400	360	Retained profits (all profit is retained)	300	380
Motor vehicles at cost	30	20	Debenture loan	400	300
Current assets:			Current liabilities:		
Stock	350	400	Creditors	300	280
Debtors	40	220	Accruals	50	60
Bank balance	30	20			
	1,650	1,870		1,650	1,870

If the balance sheets are compared item by item we have:

1. Ordinary shares £600,000–£850,000, an increase of £250,000, which is a source of funds as ordinary share capital is a liability. More money has been raised by the issue of shares.
2. Retained profits £300,000–£380,000, an increase of £80,000, which is a source of funds. More profit has been made.
3. Debenture loan £400,000 decreased to £300,000, a decrease of £100,000, which is a use of funds—£100,000 of the borrowing has been repaid.
4. Creditors £300,000 decreased to £280,000, a decrease of £20,000, which is a use of funds—£20,000 of creditors have been repaid.
5. Accrual £50,000—£60,000, an increase of £10,000. This is a source of funds. Electricity has been received (or gas or beneficial occupation obtained) for which payment has not been made.
6. Land and buildings at cost, that is ignoring depreciation, £800,000–£850,000 an increase of £50,000, which is a use of funds as land and buildings are an asset. Expenditure has taken place on additional land and buildings.
7. Plant and machinery £400,000 decreased to £360,000, a decrease of £40,000, which is a source of funds—£40,000 of plant and machinery has been sold off.
8. Motor vehicles £30,000 decreased to £20,000, a decrease of £10,000, which is a source of funds—£10,000 of motor vehicles have been sold off.
9. Stocks £350,000—£400,000, an increase of £50,000, which is a use of funds—£50,000 of additional stock has been purchased.
10. Debtors £40,000—£220,000, an increase of £180,000, which is a use of funds—£180,000 of additional credit has been extended to customers.
11. Bank balance £30,000 decreased to £20,000, a decrease of £10,000, which is a source of funds. The business has failed to generate sufficient funds for its needs and has made up the deficit by employing some of its bank balance.

One way of preparing the complete funds flow statement may be illustrated as:

Funds flow statement
for the year ending 30 June 1991

	£'000s	£'000s
Sources:		
Ordinary share capital	250	
Retained profits (ignoring depreciation)	80	
Accruals	10	
Plant and machinery	40	
Motor vehicles	10	390
Uses:		
Debenture loan	100	
Creditors	20	
Land and buildings	50	
Stocks	50	
Debtors	180	400
DEFICIT FOR YEAR		10

Deficit met by reducing the bank balance by £10,000.

This is not the only way of preparing a funds flow statement, but as it highlights the overall impact of the year's activities it is one that is often used.

In preparing it there is a basic assumption that no depreciation has been charged against profit. This would not normally be the case and where depreciation has been charged it has to be added back to profit in preparing the funds flow statement. This is because depreciation reduces profit without using any funds. It is merely an adjustment of figures.

The statement shows clearly that although an additional £250,000 has been raised by the issue of shares and £80,000 profit, there is a deficit or shortfall of £10,000. This is due largely to the repayment of the loan of £100,000 and the additional credit of £180,000 extended to customers. It would be interesting to explore this further. If the difficult economic climate has made it necessary to offer much greater credit to customers in order to maintain the same level of sales there could very soon be a cash flow problem. If, on the other hand, the credit has been extended to increase sales vastly and achieve greater market penetration then it could well be that there is no problem in this area at all. However, there is a definite need to investigate the debtor figure more fully. If it is purely a result of poor credit control, then there is a serious problem that must be rectified at once. It may be possible to renew the £100,000 debenture loan but it is unlikely that money could be raised by the issues of shares in the current year.

The funds flow statement, read in conjunction with the income statement and balance sheet, reveals a great deal about an organization and, if you read four years together, you can see clearly whether the organization is expanding, contracting or virtually hibernating.

SOURCE AND DISPOSAL OF FUNDS STATEMENT QUESTION

6.1 Prepare the relevant source and disposal of funds statements.

Balance sheet

	Cost £	Depreciation £	Dec 1990 £	June 1991 £	Dec 1991 £
Fixed assets					
Dec 90	200,000	50,000	150,000		
June 91	210,000	52,000		158,000	
Dec 91	235,000	55,000			180,000
Current assets:					
Stock			60,000	70,000	90,000
Debtors			60,000	70,000	77,000
Cash			55,000	20,000	6,000
			325,000	318,000	353,000

	Dec 1990 £	June 1991 £	Dec 1991 £
Ordinary share capital	100,000	100,000	100,000
Reserves	60,000	60,000	60,000
Profit and loss account	40,000	52,000	50,000
6 per cent debentures	200,000	212,000	210,000
Sundry liabilities	50,000	50,000	50,000
Creditors	50,000	48,000	55,000
Provision for taxation	10,000	8,000	18,000
Provision for dividend	15,000	—	20,000
	325,000	318,000	353,000

The company made a profit before taxation of £20,000 Jan–June 1991
£28,000 July–Dec 1991

Company sales were: Half-year to Dec 90 £120,000
Half-year to June 91 £145,000
Half-year to Dec 91 £165,000

SOLUTION

Funds flow statement
(sources—disposal of funds statement)
December 1990 to June 1991

6.1

	£'000s	£'000s
Sources:		
Retained profit	12	
Depreciation	2	14
	—	
Uses:		
Creditors	2	
Tax provision	2	
Dividend provision	15	
Fixed assets	10	
Stock	10	
Debtors	10	49
	—	—
DEFICIT		35
		=

Deficit met by reducing cash balance from
£55,000 to £20,000.

June 1991 to December 1991

	£'000s	£'000s
Sources:		
Taxation provision	10	
Dividend provision	20	
Depreciation	3	
Creditors	7	40
	—	
Uses:		
Loss	2	
Creditors	—	
Fixed assets	25	
Stock	20	
Debtors	7	54
	—	—
DEFICIT		14
		=

Deficit met by reducing cash balance from
£20,000 to £6,000.

December 1990 to December 1991

	£'000s	£'000s
Sources:		
Retained profit	10	
Depreciation	5	
Creditors	5	
Taxation provision	8	
Dividend provision	5	33
	—	
Uses:		
Increased fixed assets	35	
Increased stock	30	
Increased debtors	17	82
	—	—
DEFICIT		49
		=

Deficit met by reducing cash from £55,000 to £6,000.

The profitable running of the business for a year has resulted in an overall reduction in cash of £49,000. This has been caused primarily by an increase in fixed assets of £35,000 and increased stock of £30,000. It may be a sign that the business is expanding and has bought more fixed assets and stock to allow this to happen. On the other hand it may indicate that the original fixed assets have been overtaken by the pace of technological change and have had to be replaced. The build-up of stock and the increased debtors could be due to a failure to sell in the market place. There is not sufficient information to decide which suggestion is correct but clearly further investigation is necessary. It is clear that the main increase in fixed assets and stock occurred in the second half of the year and may indicate that things are happening at an accelerating pace, which would be an indication of the need for careful management.

CHAPTER SEVEN

COSTING

We have seen that the financial accounts in the form of the income statement, balance sheet and funds flow statement provide much useful information that is made even more meaningful when the appropriate ratios are sensibly employed. In today's fast-changing environment management requires even more detailed information in order to help facilitate decision making and control. It is for this reason that costing, the process of analysing the expenditure of a business unit into the separate costs for each of the products or services which the business supplies to its customers, came into being.

The cost accounts, while providing more detailed information than the financial accounts, do not stand alone. To be meaningful they must be reconciled with the financial accounts on a frequent basis, preferably monthly. The way in which the cost and financial accounts are reconciled may be illustrated simply as follows:

Financial accounts

	£'000s
Revenues	485
Expenses	300
PROFIT	185

Cost accounts

	£'000s	£'000s	£'000s	£'000s
Product	A	B	C	Total
Revenue	250	130	105	485
Expenses	200	90	10	300
PROFIT	50	40	95	185

Without the benefit of cost accounts management may have been unaware of the performance of product C. The accounts reconcile with one another; if they did not do so there would be little point in preparing them.

The aims of costing can be summarized as:

1. To provide information for effective decision making. However, it will not make the decision for you.
2. To provide the basis of pricing policies, estimates and tenders. It should be borne in mind that price is generally dependent on what the market will bear rather than on costs.
3. To maintain operational control over the activities of the organization and in particular its costs. This is considered by many to be the primary aim of costing and standard costing has been developed specifically for this purpose.
4. To enable valuations of work in progress and finished stock to be made for short-term and annual trading accounts.

Costs consist of three elements which are further divided into direct costs and indirect costs. The three elements are:
1. Labour costs
2. Material costs
3. Overhead costs or expenses

Direct labour costs are the wages of those employees who are actually building the product. Indirect labour costs are the wages of those employees who are not actually building the product, like cleaners or foremen.

Direct material costs are the costs of those materials actually consumed in the building of the product and which become a tangible part of the product. Indirect material costs are those materials that are not incorporated in the product, like oil for lubricating machinery and cleaning cloth.

Direct overhead costs are the costs of services applied directly to the product like electro-plating. Indirect overhead costs are all production, administration, distribution and selling expenses not specific to a unit of the product, e.g., rent and rates. The cost accounts are amalgamated in the financial accounts to enable their preparation in the following way:

    Direct labour
+ Direct materials
+ Direct expense
= PRIME COST
+ Factory overhead
= PRODUCTION COST
+ Selling and distribution overhead
+ Selling and distribution direct expenses
+ Administrative overhead
= COST OF SALES taken from SELLING PRICE
= NET PROFIT

Before the above information can be prepared the relevant costs have to be collected. In the case of labour and materials the collection of the data may be achieved fairly readily but so far as overhead costs for a period are concerned it is much more difficult to achieve.

Labour costs are recovered on the basis of the time used on an operation and this information is readily available from time sheets and job cards. Direct labour is charged to order numbers that refer to individual jobs so that the labour cost for each job may be collected. Indirect labour is charged to expense codes or standing order numbers which relate to a particular type and location of overhead expense.

Material costs are calculated from the material requisition or the bill for materials, copies of which are sent to the finance section. Material issues are most commonly priced using one of the following methods:

1. *Specific price*. This is used for material that has been bought for a specific job and sometimes in small concerns that hold little stock.
2. *First in first out (FIFO)*. This is used where it can be assumed that the stock is turned over regularly. The issues are always made from the stock that has been held for the longest time. The price charged is that of the longest held stock.
3. *Average price*. This is frequently used where accounts are computerized. Each time supplies are received an average price is calculated and employed until the next receipt of supplies. The price is calculated on the following basis:

$$\frac{(\text{Qty recd} \times \text{actual price}) + (\text{Qty in stock} \times \text{previous average price})}{\text{Quantity received} + \text{Quantity in stock}}$$

4. *Standard price*. This prices stocks and issues at the predetermined standard, any difference is immediately charged to an account that contains the differences or variances called the material price variance account.

Direct materials are charged to the job order numbers while indirect materials go to expense code numbers.

There must be a physical reconciliation between the amounts received into and issues from stock and the amounts paid for on invoices and charged to work done.

Overhead costing is concerned with charging the indirect expenses of production, administration, selling and distribution to the product or service provided by the business. The overhead cost is usually more significant than either direct wages or direct materials.

Where the level of overhead is considered to be sufficiently different in different parts of the business it is divided up into cost centres. Each cost centre has overhead costs built around it which can be separately totalled. A cost centre may be a whole factory, a department, a group of people, a specialized piece of equipment or a group of machines.

There are many ways of charging overheads to a cost centre and the following are some of them:

1. Actual—this is suitable for indirect wages
2. Floorspace—suitable for rent and rates
3. Number of employees—suitable for canteen costs
4. HP of machinery—electricity
5. Wattage of equipment—electricity

The overhead cost of each cost centre can then be recovered on the products passing through the cost centre on the most appropriate basis.

7.1 COSTING METHODS

Absorption costing, which is fully discussed in Chapter 8, takes account of the full cost of providing the goods or services. There is another approach, which will be explored in Chapter 11, on costing for decision making, called marginal costing. This takes account of the variable cost of products and excludes fixed costs from the decision-making process.

Job and process costing are two other methods used to fill specific needs. The examples used in Chapter 8 are of job costing, employed when it is necessary to arrive at the cost of a job or operation. They can employ either the total cost or marginal cost approach, depending on the philosophy of the organization in which they are employed. Process costing is used where production goes ahead as a continuous flow and is not broken down into discrete units. Examples may be in chemical manufacture or petroleum products. There may well be separate processes or stages before the final product and each of these stages is treated as a separate cost centre around which costs may be collected. Job and process costing are very similar to one another and which is chosen depends entirely on the operation being undertaken by the organization.

The final costing system that will be discussed is standard costing. The job costing in Chapter 8 is based on actual labour and material costs, whereas a standard costing system would be based on forecast or expected costs. This enables the actual costs to be compared with the expected costs and the differences (variances) analysed. Standard costing is an extremely effective system of control when correctly employed by management and is fully integrated with and reconcilable to the financial operating system. It is discussed in Chapter 9.

Whichever costing system is employed, actual or standard, and the costing method used in conjunction with them, it should be remembered that no two businesses are the same and what is suitable for one is unlikely to be suitable for another. Even the same business changes over time so the usefulness of the costing information that is being provided should be regularly and frequently reviewed.

EIGHT

OVERHEAD COSTS

Overhead/absorption costing, as has already been stated, takes account of the full cost of providing goods or services and ensures that the cost centres absorb the relevant costs. There are several ways of doing this and any of the following is quite acceptable.

8.1 PERCENTAGE METHODS

Percentage of direct wages If, for example, the total direct wage bill for a period is expected to be £100,000 and the total overheads allocated to that cost centre for the same period is £500,000, then each £1 direct wages will also have to recover £5 of overheads if they are all to be recovered. That is, if a job takes 10 minutes and has a direct labour cost of £2 then £10 of overheads will also have to be charged to that job. Therefore, the overheads are 500 per cent of direct wages.

Percentage of direct materials In this case the overheads of £500,000 would be expressed as a percentage of the expected cost of direct materials for the year. If this was £50,000 then the percentage would be 1,000 per cent of direct materials. Every £1 of direct materials would need to have £10 added to it to recover overhead costs.

Percentage of prime cost The same process would be followed as before except that in this case the percentage would be added to the prime cost. That is, direct materials and direct labour.

8.2 HOURLY METHODS

Labour hour rate If the total anticipated labour hours for a period are known and the total overhead cost for the cost centre has been calculated it is possible to arrive at a labour hour rate for the period. For example, if the total labour hours are 10,000 and the overheads to be recovered through that cost centre are £500,000 for the same period, then the labour hour rate will be £500,000 ÷ 10,000 = £50. That is to say the direct labour hour spent on an operation will have to recover £50 overheads.

Machine hour rate   This is calculated in exactly the same way as the labour hour rate except machine hours replace labour hours.

8.3 UNIT METHOD

This is employed where only one product uses the cost centre. The total units that will be produced are estimated and divided into the overheads for the period, which gives the total overheads to be recovered by each unit. For example, if total units to be produced is 400 and the overheads are £500,000, each unit must recover £500,000 ÷ 400 = £1,250 of overheads.

To hasten the provision of information, labour and materials are normally charged at actual cost and overhead at a predetermined recovery rate. A periodical reconciliation between actual costs and overhead recovered is essential to ensure that the estimated and actual costs bear a close relation to one another.

8.4 ACTIVITY METHOD: ACTIVITY BASED COSTING (ABC)

Recent debates have accentuated the difference between the legal requirements of furnishing financial information for tax and reporting purposes, and the needs of management for accurate costs to aid good decision making. It is felt that the labour or machine hours methods of apportioning overheads to products may not be sufficiently relevant to provide good information for decision making and control. To provide relevant information speedily a new approach to the allocation of overheads based on activity cost pools is advocated. The suggested approach may be compared with the absorption costing methods diagrammatically as shown in Figures 8.1 and 8.2.

This is felt to give relevant information speedily to management thus helping decision making and control. Activity based costing is already successfully employed in Europe, America and Japan and it is anticipated that it will in time replace the traditional method of absorption costing.

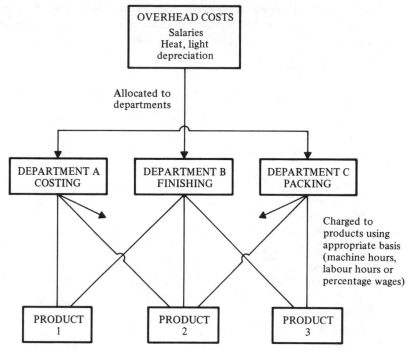

Figure 8.1 Absorption Costing

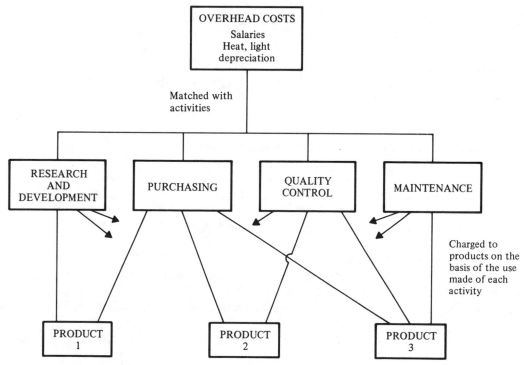

Figure 8.2 Activity Based Costing

Cost calculations must be reviewed frequently. When a cost has been arrived at it is only true for further production under the same conditions, the same price levels and the same activity levels. Let us now work through the example below which illustrates some of the ways in which overhead costs may be recovered.

From the following information calculate the cost of Job No. 1:

Prime/direct costs of Job No. 1		*Machine hours*
Direct materials	£1,000	
Direct wages		
Press shop @ £12 per hr	10 hr	17
Machine shop @ £15 per hr	25 hr	90
Machine shop @ £11 per hr	8 hr	
Assembly shop @ £12 per hr	60 hr	6

The estimated total hours for the year are:

Direct labour		
Press shop 30,000 hr @ £12 per hr		60,000
Machine shop 45,000 hr @ £15 per hr		180,000
Machine shop 12,000 hr @ £11 per hr		
Assembly shop 113,000 hr @ £12 per hr		10,000

Estimated overheads for the year:

	£	*Basis of apportionment*
Indirect labour	500,000	Direct labour hours
Salaries	200,000	Direct labour hours
Depreciation	40,000	Plant valuation
Maintenance	20,000	As given (budget)
Rent, rates	60,000	Floor area

The following information relates to the respective shops:

	Press shop	*Machine shop*	*Assembly shop*
Plant valuation	£200,000	£150,000	£50,000
Floor area	6,000 sq. ft	9,000 sq. ft	5,000 sq. ft
Maintenance	£7,000	£5,000	£8,000

Calculate the cost of Job No. 1.

In calculating the cost we first need to discover how much of the annual overhead it should carry. To do so we apportion the overhead between the three shops on the suggested basis. There is no set way of laying out this calculation but one method would be:

	Press shop £	Machine shop £	Assembly shop £
Indirect labour	75,000	142,500	282,500
Salaries	30,000	57,000	113,000
Depreciation	20,000	15,000	5,000
Maintenance	7,000	5,000	8,000
Rent and rates	18,000	27,000	15,000
TOTAL	150,000	246,500	423,500
Direct labour hr	30,000	57,000	113,000
Labour hr rate	£5	£4.32	£3.75
Machine hr	60,000	180,000	10,000
Machine hr rate	£2.50	£1.37	£42.35
Direct wages	£360,000	£807,000	£1,356,000
Direct wages (%)	41.67%	30.55%	31.23%

The prime or direct cost of Job No. 1 will be the same whichever method is employed to recover overheads.

Prime/direct cost of Job No. 1

	£	£
Labour		
Press shop 10 hr @ £12 per hr =	120	
Machine shop 25 hr @ £15 per hr =	375	
Machine shop 8 hr @ £11 per hr =	88	
Assembly shop 60 hr @ £12		
per hr =	720	
	1,303	
Materials	1,000	
PRIME/DIRECT COST		2,303

Overhead Cost

1. Using labour hr to recover overheads

Press shop 10 hr @ £5 per hr	=	50.00	
Machine shop 33 hr @ £4.32 per hr	=	142.56	
Assembly shop 60 hr @ £3.75 per hr	=	225.00	
			417.56

TOTAL COST OF JOB NO. 1   £2,720.56

2. Using machine hr to recover overheads		£	£
Press shop 17 hr @ £2.50	=	42.50	
Machine shop 90 hr @ £1.37	=	123.30	
Assembly shop 6 hr @ £42.35	=	254.10	
		————	
Total overhead cost			419.90
Add Prime cost			2,303.00
			————
TOTAL COST OF JOB NO. 1			£2,722.90

3. Using percentage of direct wages			
Press shop 41.67% of £120	=	50.00	
Machine shop 30.55% of £463	=	141.45	
Assembly shop 31.23% of £720	=	224.86	
Total overhead cost		———	416.31
Add Prime cost			2,303.00
			————
TOTAL COST OF JOB NO. 1			£2,719.31

Each different method of recovering overheads gives a slightly different answer, but they are all in the same region and will even out over the period. It is important to remember that the calculation gives the cost of the job and includes no profit element. If similar firms are charging £1,500 for this type of work you will have serious problems as it is extremely unlikely that anyone could be persuaded to pay you £3,000. The price that you charge will be very largely decided by what the market will bear and not what it costs you to make. If your production process is about right you might in an expanding economy be able to charge £4,000 for the job and make a reasonable profit. In a poor economic climate you may be pleased to keep your workforce employed and charge £2,500, so that you cover your prime costs and get a contribution to your overhead cost. This concept will be further discussed in Chapter 12 on costing for decision making.

Costing example An engineering company makes scale models in two types, standard and de luxe. Three departments are involved in manufacturing the product—casting, finishing and packing.

Costs and expenses incurred in quarter 1

	Casting £	Finishing £	Packing £	TOTAL £
Apportioned company admin.				3,000
Clerical and indirect wages				2,250
Maintenance of equipment				900
Management salaries				2,000
Depreciation of equipment				1,800
Rent and rates				480
Expense supplies				375
Direct materials	3,600	400	800	4,800
Direct wages	2,000	4,000	4,000	10,000
Labour hours	400 hr	800 hr	800 hr	2,000 hr

The total output for the quarter was 10,000 standard and 5,000 de luxe models. The division of direct costs between the two models was:

	Casting £	Finishing £	Packing £	
Direct wages—standard	1,200	2,000	2,400	
Direct wages—de luxe	800	2,000	1,600	
Direct materials—standard	2,000	240	480	
Direct materials—de luxe	1,600	160	220	
General information				TOTAL
Floor area—sq. ft	2,000	2,000	4,000	8,000
Equipment at book value	50,000	15,000	15,000	80,000

Calculate the cost of
(a) one standard model
(b) one de luxe model

SOLUTION
Overhead apportionment

	Casting £	Finishing £	Packing £	TOTAL £
Company admin.	600	1,200	1,200	3,000
Clerical and indirect wages	450	900	900	2,250
Maintenance of equipment	562	169	169	900
Management salaries	400	800	800	2,000
Depreciation of equipment	1,125	337	338	1,800
Rent and rates	120	120	240	480
Expense supplies	75	150	150	375
	3,332	3,676	3,797	10,805
Labour hours	400	800	800	
Labour hour rate	8.33	4.59	4.75	

Direct labour hours are calculated by dividing the direct labour bills by 5 (hourly rate)

Cost of one de luxe model	£
Direct materials	1,980
Direct wages	4,400
Prime/direct cost	6,380
Overhead cost	
Casting 160 × £8.33 = 1332.8	
Finishing 400 × £4.59 = 1836	
Packing 320 × £4.75 = 1520	4,688.8
Total cost of one de luxe model	11,068.8 ÷ 5,000 = £2.21

Cost of one standard model	£
Direct materials	2,720
Direct wages	5,600
Prime/direct cost	8,320
Overhead cost	
Casting 240 × £8.33 = 1,999.2	
Finishing 400 × £4.59 = 1,836	
Packing 480 × £4.75 = 2,280	6,115.2
Total cost of one standard model	14,435.2 ÷ 10,000 = £1.44

In apportioning the overhead costs among the three departments the following steps were taken:

1. *Company administration*—apportioned on the basis of the direct labour hours. The total overhead was £3,000 and the total direct labour hours 2,000.

$$\frac{400}{2,000} \times £3,000 = £600 \text{ to casting}$$

$$\frac{800}{2,000} \times £3,000 = £1,200 \text{ to finishing}$$

$$\frac{800}{2,000} \times £3,000 = £1,200 \text{ to packing}$$

2. *Clerical and indirect wages*—apportioned on the basis of the direct wages. The total overhead was £2,250 and the total direct wages £10,000.

$$\frac{2,000}{10,000} \times £2,250 = £450 \text{ to casting}$$

$$\frac{4,000}{10,000} \times £2,250 = £900 \text{ to finishing}$$

$$\frac{4,000}{10,000} \times £2,250 = £900 \text{ to packing}$$

3. *Maintenance of equipment*—apportioned on the basis of the book value of the equipment and rounded off to the nearest £1. The total overhead was £900 and the total value of equipment £80,000.

$$\frac{50,000}{80,000} \times £900 = £562.5 = £562 \text{ to casting}$$

$$\frac{15,000}{80,000} \times £900 = £168.75 = £169 \text{ to finishing}$$

$$\frac{15,000}{80,000} \times £900 = £168.75 = £169 \text{ to packing}$$

4. *Management salaries*—apportioned on the basis of the direct labour hours. The total overhead was £2,000 and the total direct labour hours 2,000.

$$\frac{400}{2,000} \times £2,000 = £400 \text{ to casting}$$

$$\frac{800}{2,000} \times £2,000 = £800 \text{ to finishing}$$

$$\frac{800}{2,000} \times £2,000 = £800 \text{ to packing}$$

5. *Depreciation of equipment*—apportioned on the basis of the book value of the equipment. The total overhead was £1,800 and the total value of equipment £80,000.

$$\frac{50,000}{80,000} \times £1,800 = £1,125 \text{ to casting}$$

$$\frac{15,000}{80,000} \times £1,800 = £337.50 = £337 \text{ to finishing}$$

$$\frac{15,000}{80,000} \times £1,800 = £337.50 = £338 \text{ to packing}$$

Note The £337.50 has been rounded up in one case and down in the other in order to ensure that the total is correct.

6. *Rent and rates*—apportioned on the basis of floor area. The total overhead was £480 and the total floor area 8,000 sq. ft.

$$\frac{2,000}{8,000} \times £480 = £120 \text{ to casting}$$

$$\frac{2,000}{8,000} \times £480 = £120 \text{ to finishing}$$

$$\frac{4,000}{8,000} \times £480 = £240 \text{ to packing}$$

7. *Expense supplies*—apportioned on the basis of direct labour hours. The total overhead was £375 and the total direct labour hours 2,000.

$$\frac{400}{2,000} \times £375 = £75 \text{ to casting}$$

$$\frac{800}{2,000} \times £375 = £150 \text{ to finishing}$$

$$\frac{800}{2,000} \times £375 = £150 \text{ to packing}$$

This is not the only way to tackle the question and other methods of recovering overheads may be preferred. Whichever method is used it will never be completely accurate and it is essential to carry out frequent reconciliations between the actual and budgeted (expected) figures.

NINE

STANDARD COSTING

Standard costing is based on expected costs and the first difficulty lies in deciding what costs should be expected. They will rarely if ever be 100 per cent accurate as nobody has perfect knowledge of the future. The second difficulty lies in comparing the actual with the expected costs and the third is what to do about the differences where they are found to exist.

In setting the standard or expected costs, existing businesses have advantages over entirely new businesses because it is a little easier to forecast what you think will happen in the future if you know what has happened over the last three or four years. For both existing and new businesses, however, the forecasts should be based on all the available relevant information. Market research surveys should be undertaken and balanced with views on the likely economic environment to arrive at the activity level. When this has been done, wherever possible there should be a spread of at least three outcomes—most optimistic, most pessimistic and most likely to be achieved.

The behavioural impact of a good standard costing system cannot be overemphasized. It is one of the few ways in which the performance of individuals may be measured. For this reason great care must be exercised in arriving at the standard or norm. It is of little use to either the organization or the individuals within it to set a standard that is too easily obtained as this will lead to under-performance and frustration. At first there will be a feeling of satisfaction at having achieved the targets, but as this is repeated period after period, with increasing ease, boredom will set in and staff concerned will become disillusioned and demotivated to the detriment of the organization.

The setting of a standard that is too difficult to attain will be equally detrimental to both staff and organization. Staff that have been carefully recruited will at first be highly motivated and make every effort to achieve the targets set. With each accounting period it will become more obvious that the targets cannot be achieved and, gradually, staff will become demotivated until they finally give up the unequal struggle. Once they have become demoralized, it is difficult to restore people's faith in the management of the organization. In view of this it is better to avoid this situation altogether by setting targets that are obtainable, but only when people are working at a high level of efficiency.

This is easy to state but difficult to achieve. How do we set standards that are achievable only after the expenditure of effort and the use of initiative? To use last year's standards inflated by 5 per cent for the current year achieves little, since errors and slack in all probability were built into last year's figures. To employ a method study approach, and state that in perfect conditions an operation can be done in two hours, and set this as the standard will not work either. We have somehow to find ways of eliminating the errors and building in sufficient slack to allow for the abilities of the personnel who are carrying out the work. If this can be done with any degree of accuracy the organization will become more efficient and the people in it obtain greater satisfaction from their work.

Costs, as we have seen, can be broken down into labour, materials and overheads. It is possible to set a standard for each of these elements and to compare it with the actual cost periodically, e.g., weekly or monthly. This enables action to be taken where the actual cost differs from the expected. For the standard costing system to be really useful it is necessary to analyse the costs a little further than labour, materials and overheads.

9.1 PRINCIPAL VARIANCES EMPLOYED IN COSTING

Materials

1. *Material price variance*. This is caused by changes in the purchase prices of the materials used. This variance is calculated by using the formula:

   Actual quantity (Standard price – Actual price)

2. *Material usage variance*. This is caused by using more or less material than the standard quantity and the formula used to calculate it is:

   Standard price (Standard usage – Actual usage)

   Example
   Standard—8 metres of material @ £2 a metre = £16 per unit
   Actual—820 metres of material @ £2.10 a metre = £1,722 per 100 units
   Price variance = (820 × 10p) = £82 adverse

that is, actual usage × price change. It is adverse because the price has increased. It is greater than standard. An adverse variance shows that costs are greater than expected whereas a favourable variance shows they are less than expected.

   Usage variance = (20 × £2) = £40 adverse

that is, change in use × standard price. It is adverse because the use has increased. For 100 units you would have expected to use 800 metres (8 × 100 units) and have in fact used 820 metres. The total materials variance is £122 adverse which is (£82 + £40) and equals actual £1,722 − standard £1,600 (16 × 100 units).

Labour

1. *Labour rate variance*. This is caused by changes in the wage rates. The formula to calculate this is:

Actual hours (Standard wage rate per hour – Actual wage rate per hour)

2. *Labour efficiency variance*. This is caused by the speed of production being greater or less than the standard speed. The formula employed is:

Standard wage rate per hour (Standard hours worked – Actual hours worked)

Example
Standard—2 hr @ £5 per hour = £10 per unit
Actual—190 hr @ £5.40 per hour = £1,026 per 100 units
Rate variance = (£190 × 40p) = £76 adverse

that is, change in rate × actual hours. It is adverse because the rate has increased. It is 40p greater than standard.

Efficiency variance = (10 × £5) = £50 favourable

It is favourable because for 100 units you would expect to use 200 hours but have only used 190 hours.

Total labour variance is £26 adverse

which is (£76 – £50) and equals 1,026 – 1,000 (£10 × 100 units).

Overhead

1. *Expenditure variance*. This is caused by spending more or less than that allowed by the standard.
To calculate this we use this formula:

(Actual hours at standard cost – Actual hours at actual cost)

2. *Efficiency*. This is caused by the speed of production being greater or less than the standard or expected speed.
This uses the formula:

(Actual production – Standard production) Standard overhead per unit

3. *Capacity*. This is caused by working more or less hours than the standard working hours. The formula used is:

(Actual hours – Expected hours) Fixed overhead per hour

Example
Standard overhead cost is £4 per unit, based on a four-week capacity of 600 units in 200 working hours with an allowed expenditure £2,400 on overheads, of which £800 is fixed and £1,600 is variable with the time worked. Actual results were 660 units produced in 240 hours at a cost of £2,600.

Expenditure variance = (£800 + £1,920) – £2,600 = £120 favourable that is, the expected expenditure for that level of activity of £800 fixed + (£8 variable with time × 240 hours = £1,920) less the actual cost of £2,600.

Efficiency variance = (720 units − 660 units) × £4 = £240 adverse

that is, the expected production of three units per hour × the 240 hours equals 720 units *less* the actual output 660. The difference is multiplied by £4 per unit standard overhead cost. Fewer units than expected have been produced so there is an adverse difference (variance) as we have fewer units over which to spread our costs.

Capacity variance = 40 hours × £4 = £160 favourable

that is, the actual hours of 240 − expected hours of 200 and the difference is multiplied by the fixed overhead cost per hour. More than the expected hours have been worked so we have a favourable variance.

The total variance is (£120 + £160) favourable − £240 adverse = £40 favourable

This ties in with the total overhead variance which is:

$$
\begin{array}{lr}
\text{Expected cost of 660 units } (660 \times 4) = & \text{£2,640} \\
\text{Actual cost of 660 units} \quad\quad\quad\quad = & \text{£2,600} \\
\hline
\text{Total variance} \quad\quad\quad\quad\quad & \text{£40 favourable} \\
\end{array}
$$

Having calculated these variances what use can we make of them? The materials variance is broken down into material price and material usage, each of which may be either controllable or non-controllable as far as the management of the undertaking is concerned.

Material price variance

If this is caused by a nationally agreed change in the price of the materials used in production or providing a service or because the original standard was wrong, management can only accept the price change and use it to explain the difference between the standard and actual. This is an explainable variance which will be repeated in each period until it is possible to set the new standard cost. Where the price variance is caused because material of a higher or lower quality than necessary is being used, action can be taken to ensure that material of the correct quality is purchased from the right supplier.

Material usage variance

If this is caused because the original estimate was wrong, management can only accept the usage variance and use it to explain the difference between the standard and the actual, in which case it will remain an explainable variance until the new standard can be established. Where it is caused by materials of the wrong quality, action can be taken to ensure that material of the correct quality is obtained. If the difference is caused because new staff are being trained, then it will be an explainable variance until the training is complete when the material usage should revert to normal.

The labour variance is broken down into labour rate and labour efficiency, each of which may be either controllable or non-controllable as far as management is concerned.

Labour rate variance

If this is caused by a nationally agreed change in the wage rate or because the standard was wrong, management can only accept it as an explainable variance until the standard can be altered. Where it is caused by using labour that is either too highly skilled or not yet skilled enough, management can take action to ensure that labour of the correct calibre is employed.

Labour efficiency variance

If this is caused by an incorrect standard, management can only accept it as an explainable variance until the new standard is established. Where it is caused by variances in the quality of material, making the work either more or less difficult, steps should be taken to ensure that material of the correct quality is obtained. Where it is caused by using staff who are more or less highly trained than is necessary to perform the task satisfactorily, the correct staff should be employed. Where it is caused through demotivated staff, then a serious problem exists that will have to be handled extremely carefully.

Overhead variances

These should be monitored in the same way as the other variances so that those concerned are aware of their existence. There is little that management can do, however, to correct them in the short term.

Before anything can be done about any of the variances the organization has to be aware that they exist. This necessitates an efficient system of financial control and reporting that presents the required information promptly and in a readily understandable form. Providing the information serves no useful purpose unless it is acted upon vigorously and punctually. Failure to do so will allow the situation continually to deteriorate until it may become too late to correct it and save the organization.

Standard costing involves comparing actual costs with estimated, forecast or budgeted costs and refers to a small part of the organization which may be a job, a department, a factory or a machine. Budgetary control employs exactly the same principles as standard costing but relates it to the whole organization. Budgetary control is discussed in Chapter 10.

Example Davies Production Company makes fuel packs which are sold in dozen packs to the retail trade at £6 per pack. The standard cost of a dozen packs is:

Manufacturing		£
Materials 4lb @ 20p per lb	=	0.80
Labour 1 hr @ £3.00 per hr	=	3.00
Overhead (based on a 40 hr 10,000 production hr week with production set at 10,000 dozen and budgeted expenditure—£12,000)	=	1.20
Selling		
Salary and commission	=	0.40
		———
TOTAL STANDARD COST	=	£5.40

The actual costs in period 10 (four-week period) were as follows:

		£
Material 220,000 lb @ 20.5p per lb	=	45,100
Labour 47,000 hours @ £3.10	=	145,700
Overhead	=	49,500
Selling costs	=	16,500
		———
TOTAL	=	256,800

In period 10 the sales and production totalled 50,000 dozen packs, all sold at the full wholesale price.

SUGGESTED SOLUTION

Normal profit and loss account—Period 10

	£	£
Sales		300,000
Cost of sales:		
Materials	45,100	
Labour	145,700	
Manufacturing overhead	49,500	240,300
	———	———
		59,700
Selling costs		16,500
		———
NET PROFIT		43,200

Standard cost profit and loss account—Period 10

	£	£
Sales		300,000
Less standard cost of sales		270,000
Standard profit on sales		30,000
Add FAVOURABLE VARIANCES		
Labour efficiency	9,000	
Selling costs	3,500	
Overhead	10,500	23,000
		53,000
Less ADVERSE VARIANCES		
Material price	1,100	
Material usage	4,000	
Wage rate	4,700	9,800
NET PROFIT		£43,200

Labour efficiency variance £

3,000 hours × £3   =   9,000 favourable

Selling costs variance

Expected 50,000 × 40p = 20,000

Actual   = 16,500   3,500 favourable

Material price variance

220,000 lb × £0.005   =   1,100 adverse

Material usage variance

20,000 lb × £0.2   =   4,000 adverse

Labour rate variance

47,000 lb × £0.1   =   4,700 adverse

Overhead variance

Expected (50,000 × £1.2) = 60,000

Actual   = 49,500   10,500 favourable

The variances are calculated in the manner shown. In each case the actual performance is compared with the expected performance and the differences reported. It is important that they are acted upon as well as reported. Modern business is complex and there is insufficient time to act upon every variance that occurs so some differences cannot be investigated. Once it has been decided what is an acceptable variance, say, up to 15 per cent deviation from standard, those that exceed it must be promptly investigated and acted upon. It is as bad to be underspent as it is to be overspent.

BUDGETARY CONTROL

We have seen that standard costing, when properly used, is an effective method of control that can be applied to small parts of an organization. Budgetary control uses exactly the same principles but applies them to the whole organization. In budgetary control, as in standard costing, expected levels of activity are arrived at and the actual performance is compared with the expected performance. The differences between the actual activity level and expected activity level, termed variances, are reported and, where it is felt to be necessary, investigated.

10.1 THE BUDGETARY PROCESS

The budgetary process is long drawn out, often taking nine to twelve months to prepare and can be illustrated as shown in Figure 10.1.

The corporate objectives may be to maximize profit, to maximize cash flow, to achieve greatest market share, to provide the best service, to have the best product, to have the happiest employee relations, to enjoy a good public image, to provide the best possible working conditions or any combination of these or other objectives. Whatever they are they will not be arrived at instantaneously and the culture of the organization will have much to do with the final choice. It will generally be made by a small group of top executives. Existing organizations may find it difficult to change their objectives while new ones may find it hard to arrive at the objectives of the organization for the next ten years. Once objectives have been set they should not be treated as sacrosanct. Conditions are changing at an ever-increasing rate, and if organizations are to survive they must be amenable to altering their objectives as the need arises. The personality of the dominant character in the group of executives will have a big impact on the decision. Generally, if the accountant is dominant, the approach will be more constrained than would be the case if a marketing man were to prevail. The objectives having been set, a long-range plan has to be prepared to try to ensure that they are achieved. This is often for ten years into the future, with annual reviews to see that the plan is kept under control and not allowed to become meaningless. The first year is firm, the next three years firm but subject to change, and the last six tentative. The plan is subject to change when it is five years or more into the future, but it is much better to have a plan than to drift with no sense of direction at all. To have no plan is an infallible recipe for disaster.

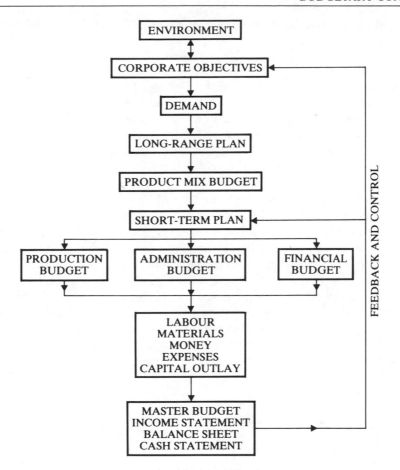

Figure 10.1 Total Budgetary Process

The sales plan should be derived from the long-term demand and the information obtained from marketing surveys and other research carried out by people in touch with existing and prospective customers. From this the product mix strategy will be decided upon and the plan for the year set. That is, the sales of each product that are expected to be achieved during the next 12 months, which will enable the individual budgets to be prepared that lead to the master budget. This will tell you how the cash situation will stand on a monthly or weekly basis over the next 12 months, what profit will be made or loss incurred, and the overall business position in the same period. Actual figures can be compared with the expected and, where necessary, the budget altered or corrective action taken. It is worth noting that while budgets are expressed in pounds (£) it is only at the very last stage that this occurs. The accountant does not prepare the budget, he simply expresses other people's ideas in terms that are universally accepted and understood. The process has to be fully integrated or it will not work. It is of little use to decide on a product mix strategy that asks for 10,000 units of A, 4,000 units of B, and 15,000 units of C if limited materials make it possible to produce only 10,000 units of A and nothing else; or to plan to make 10,000 units of A if only 2,000 units can be sold. For the budget to succeed it must be fully supported and integrated. The best way for this to be achieved is by involving as many of those who will have a role in the successful use of the budget in discussions as early as possible in the budget process.

People who have limits imposed upon them with no explanation are, generally speaking, not committed to making them work. The organization that obtains the best results from budgeting is the one that involves its people at an early stage and, so far as possible, ensures that their ideas are treated seriously and incorporated in the budget. However, there are those who do not wish to be involved in the budgetary process and resent efforts to involve them. To do so would be to court disaster. In this, as in every other case, it is dangerous to generalize and each occasion should be treated on merit. A good system of budgetary control is invaluable to any organization and even a bad one is better than none at all.

The cash budget was described with the help of an example in Chapter 4. The other budgets that relate just to one year, normally called revenue budgets, are prepared in the same way; that is, every budget shown on the chart (Figure 10.2) except the capital budget, which is treated differently and will be described in a separate chapter. Once the corporate objectives and long-range plan have been prepared and the budgeting process starts in more detail, there is usually a part which is restricting the others. It may be that a shortage of material, men or money or the sales potential could be causing concern. Whichever it is, it restricts the operation of the organization and is called the limiting factor. In most organizations today there are two areas vying for this distinction, the cash situation and the sales potential. The one that is limiting activity is chosen as the starting point for the annual budget, which is then built around it. This process may be illustrated as shown in Figure 10.2.

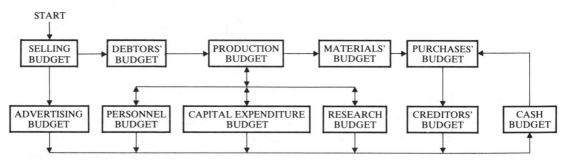

Figure 10.2   Budgetary Control

Selling budget

The selling budget is built up from the forecasts of the sales that will be made of each of the products over the next 12 months. The sales manager will provide this from information he obtains from his sales team. In smaller organizations the owner will decide on the basis of just what his sales are likely to be over the next year.

Debtors' budget

This will depend on the proportion of sales that are for cash. In a purely cash sales organization like Tesco plc there should be few people owing money to the business. If sales are low, one way to increase them may be to extend further credit facilities to customers. The debtors' budget should not be allowed to get out of control as it can lead to serious cash flow problems.

Advertising budget

The advertising budget will be set at the level believed to be necessary to obtain the required sales.

Production budget

This will be set to meet the sales levels of each product and the minimum stock requirement.

Materials' budget

This depends on the production budget and stock requirements.

Purchases' budget

This refers to the purchase of parts required in the production process and is directly dependent on the materials' budget.

Creditors' budget

This is related to the purchases' budget and the credit that suppliers are prepared to advance. Generally speaking it is good sense to keep your suppliers waiting for as long as possible before paying them. Care should be taken to ensure that payment is not withheld for so long that goodwill is lost and supplies become hard to obtain on any terms other than cash.

Personnel budget

The personnel budget is decided upon by the level of activity of the whole organization as the operations to be performed depend upon the availability of suitably qualified people.

Capital expenditure budget

This looks at the needs of the organization for accommodation and plant, machinery and equipment if it is to meet its goals. It forms a large part of the spending of most organizations that has an impact over many years.

Research budget

This budget depends on the availability of resources and the product range. If the organization is to survive it must be competitive and to be competitive means that the product is continually being updated and improved through research and development.

Cash budget

The cash budget is affected by every other budget in the organization and has to be closely monitored if the organization is to avoid problems of liquidity with all its consequences.

> **Example** Davies plans to start a business making realistic model sailing dinghies from wood. He believes that he will need to keep a small stock of a dozen boats on hand and that he will be able to make ten boats per week working on his own. The wood he needs will have to be purchased four weeks in advance, and, until he is better known, he will receive no credit. His purchases will be for cash. Each boat will use a metre of wood at £10 a cubic metre, £2 of cloth for the sails, brass fitments costing £5 and miscellaneous items to the value of £2. Each boat he estimates will take him five hours to make. He considers it to be a superior product that will be very much in demand for window displays, and feels that once he becomes known there will be strong demand for his product. He hopes to market the boat at £63 to start with, which will cover the costs already mentioned together with fixed costs consisting of rates £400, electricity £200, miscellaneous £200 and salary £6 an hour. He feels that he could just survive for the first three years on an annual profit of £6,200. His customers will be given two months' credit. He intends to start his business on 1 July and meet his production target in the first week. On 1 July he will have to pay £760 for his first four weeks' materials and this payment will be repeated each month. Rates are payable in two equal instalments on 1 July and 1 January. Electricity is payable quarterly, in equal amounts, on 1 April, 1 July, 1 October and 1 January. Miscellaneous expenses are paid weekly in equal amounts and salary is paid weekly according to hours worked, expected to be 50 hours per week. Sales are expected to be none in the first month, three in the second month, six in the third month and thereafter 80 per month.
>
> Prepare for Davies his production, purchases, sales, stock and cash budgets for the first 6 months operations, together with a statement of his projected profit and a projected balance sheet. Assume he starts business with £10,000 in the business bank account. What effect would the figures arrived at have on his original plan?

SOLUTION

Production budget (units)

	Opening stock	Made	Closing
July	—	40	40
August	40	40	77
September	77	40	111
October	111	40	71
November	71	40	31
December	31	40	—

Stock budget (units)

	Opening	Made	Sold	Balance
July	—	40	—	40
August	40	40	3	77
September	77	40	6	111
October	111	40	80	71
November	71	40	80	31
December	31	40	80	(maximum 71)

Purchases budget (£)

July	760
August	760
September	760
October	760
November	760
December	760

Sales budget (units and £)

	Units	£
July	—	—
August	3	189
September	6	378
October	80	5040
November	80	5040
December	71	4473

Cash budget

	July £	Aug £	Sept £	Oct £	Nov £	Dec £
Opening	10,000	7,774	5,798	3,822	1,985	387
Sales receipts	—	—	—	189	378	5,040
	10,000	7,774	5,798	4,011	2,363	5,427
Payments						
Purchases	760	760	760	760	760	760
Salary	1,200	1,200	1,200	1,200	1,200	1,200
Rates	200	—	—	—	—	—
Electricity	50	—	—	50	—	—
Miscellaneous	16	16	16	16	16	16
	2,226	1,976	1,976	2,026	1,976	1,976
Balance c/fwd	7,774	5,798	3,822	1,985	387	3,451

Projected income statement for 6 months to 31 December

	£	£
Sales		15,120
Less materials purchased		4,560
GROSS PROFIT		10,560
Less expenses		
Salary	7,200	
Rates	200	
Electricity	100	
Miscellaneous	96	7,596
NET PROFIT		
		£2,964

The figures for the income statement have been obtained from the cash budget except for the sales figure which is made up of the three amounts actually received in the cash budget (£189 + £378 + £5,040) = £5,607, together with November and December sales which have not yet been received (80 + 71) × £63 = £9,513. The addition of the £9,513 to the £5,607 gives the total sales figure for the six months of £15,120.

Projected balance sheet as at 31 December

	£		£
Current assets:		Capital	10,000
Debtors	9,513	RESERVES	
Bank	3,451	Net profit	2,964
	£12,964		£12,964

The capital is the money Davies originally brought into the business. The profit is as shown in the budgeted income statement. The bank balance is from the balance in the cash budget and the debtors are the monies due for November and December sales as shown above. Davies's budgets reveal that he will require storage capacity for 111 boats at the end of month three which may cause him problems. He will be unable to meet demand by the end of December and could suffer a shortage of cash in November. If his sales forecast of 80 boats a month is realistic he will have to decide whether he wants to meet this demand or go for a smaller figure. His stock holding of 12 boats is unlikely to be met without increasing his rate of production which will probably entail capital expenditure as well as obtaining some help.

MARGINAL COSTING

Marginal costing is not a complete costing system but a method of focusing the attention of management on those items that can most readily be controlled in the short term. Costs are divided into fixed costs and variable costs. Fixed costs are considered to be those that are unchanged by the level of activity while variable costs vary directly with the activity level. The behaviour of the two types of cost may be illustrated as shown in Figure 11.1(a) and (b).

The fixed costs remain at £10,000 whether nothing is produced or 50,000 units, whereas the variable costs are nil when nothing is produced and £20,000 when 50,000 units are produced. The economies of scale are ignored for this purpose and a linear relationship is assumed between output and costs. The fixed costs are treated as fixed but this will apply only within limits. If, for example, demand increases above 50,000 units it may not be possible to meet it without obtaining additional buildings and machinery, in which case the fixed cost line becomes like that shown in Figure 11.2, which illustrates the changes that take place when full capacity is reached. Despite these limitations, marginal costing is an

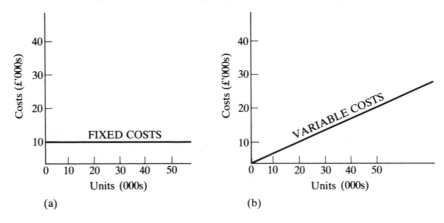

Figure 11.1 Marginal Costing

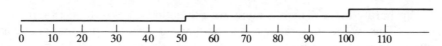

Figure 11.2 Marginal Costing

extremely useful planning tool as it assists management to prepare a scale of charges that enable different costs to be recovered. It also enables a graphical presentation of the likely impact on the business of an increase (or decrease) of sales volume using the concept of contribution. Contribution is the surplus selling price that is available to meet the fixed costs once the variable costs have been covered. For example, if a product has a selling price of £100 and variable costs of £50, then every unit sold makes a contribution of £50 towards the fixed costs and, afterwards, profit.

	£
Selling price	100
Variable cost	50
Contribution	50

In engineering circles the contribution is referred to as the gross margin.

This concept can be used to arrive at the level of sales that is necessary for the organization to break even, i.e., for total income to equal total costs. Suppose the fixed costs of the organization mentioned above are £1,000,000, then the level of sales necessary for it to break even are given by the formula:

$$\text{Break-even point} = \frac{\text{Total fixed costs}}{(\text{Selling price} - \text{variable cost}) \text{ per unit}}$$

$$= \frac{\text{Fixed costs}}{(\text{SP} - \text{VC}) \text{ per unit}}$$

$$= \frac{1,000,000}{(100 - 50)} = 20,000 \text{ units}$$

If 19,999 units are sold a loss of £50 is incurred.
If 20,001 units are sold a profit of £50 is made.
If no units are sold and made a loss of £1,000,000 is incurred.
If one unit is sold and made a loss of £999,950 is incurred.

So, it could be argued that in the short term it is better to work and sell one unit than to do nothing at all. This state of affairs could not be allowed to continue for too long but it may enable the organization to be slowly run down, or a new profitable product to be brought on line.

The concept of marginal costing is employed by, among others, British Rail, National Bus Company and the Electricity Boards when they calculate their off-peak charges to customers. They all have enormous fixed costs, and, while there are times of the day at which they can hardly meet demand, there are other times when there is a great deal of spare capacity. They would like more use to be made of this and use marginal costing in their pricing in an effort to obtain some contribution to the fixed costs. The full return fare from Fareham to Cardiff by rail may be £26 whereas an off-peak return would be, say, £18 with children travelling free. This, it is hoped, would persuade more people to use the trains that are running two-thirds empty. The charges for electricity are less at night than during normal working hours as are those for using the telephone. All this is done in an effort to get a bigger contribution to fixed costs and then, hopefully, to profit.

Contribution, or gross margin as the engineers describe it, has been discussed but an example will illustrate how it first of all covers fixed costs and then profit.

Example

Selling price £200 per unit   Variable cost £100 per unit

Total fixed costs £10,000. The projected sales in units over the next four years are:

Year	1	2	3	4
Sales	50 units	70 units	100 units	200 units

Assuming all costs and the selling price for the period remain unchanged, calculate the profit or loss in each of the four years.

SOLUTION

Year	1	2	3	4
Fixed costs	10,000	10,000	10,000	10,000
Contribution (Selling price – variable cost) × units sold	£100 × 50 5,000	£100 × 70 7,000	£100 × 100 10,000	£100 × 200 20,000
(Loss)/Profit	(5,000)	(3,000)	—	10,000

The calculations show that in years 1 and 2 the contribution is insufficient to meet the fixed costs so a loss is incurred. In year 3 the contribution is exactly equal to the fixed costs so the organization breaks even, making neither a profit nor a loss. A profit of £10,000 is made in year 4 and the business may well continue in profit if it has carefully planned its course for the next few years.

The marginal costing approach enables the break-even chart to be drawn. This is a useful planning tool as it illustrates, at a glance, the likely impact of increases or decreases in the level of sales. The axes are sales/costs in money terms against units sold (see Figure 11.3).

The example may be shown graphically (see Figures 11.3 and 11.4). In constructing the graph it is necessary to decide where the lines are to finish. This can be achieved by dropping a perpendicular at the maximum potential capacity. In this case 200 units sold. All lines will be drawn to finish against the perpendicular. The fixed cost line is drawn parallel to the base at £10,000. The total cost line (that is, the fixed + variable costs) is drawn from fixed costs £10,000 up to total costs for 200 units, that is, £10,000 + (200 × £100 variable cost) = £10,000 + £20,000 = £30,000 total cost. The total revenue line is drawn from zero up to the total revenue for 200 units sold (200 × £200) = £40,000.

The break-even point is where the total revenue and total cost lines intersect. That is, at 100 units sold. Any sales below 100 will result in a loss and any above in a profit. The magnitude of the profit or loss is given by the vertical distance between the total revenue

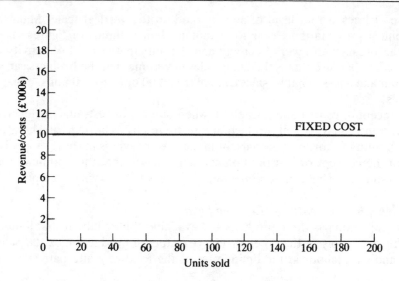

Figure 11.3   Fixed Costs Graph

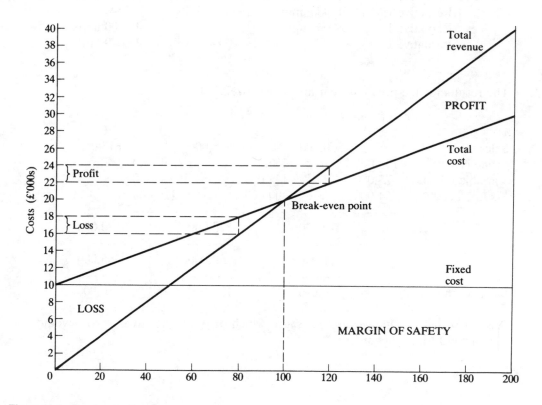

Figure 11.4   Break-even Graph

and total cost lines at that level of activity read on the vertical scale. Management often finds graphical presentation easier to assimilate than columns of figures. The difference between the break-even level of activity and the anticipated level of activity is called the margin of safety because that is the fall of sales in volume that the business can stand before it begins to make a loss. That is, sales can fall from 200 units to 100 units, a margin of safety of 100 units.

The concept of contribution is helpful when one factor restrains the level of activity in an organization. It may be that production is restricted by a shortage of labour in which case that is the limiting factor, or materials, or money. Whatever is in short supply is the limiting factor, and the concept of contribution can help ensure that the optimum use is made of available resources. This can be illustrated through the following example.

Example *Marginal costing—Limiting factor*
An organization has three products and available skilled labour that limits production. A sufficient supply of the other necessary factors of production exists. Sales demand is good and with labour as the limiting factor the following alternatives are available.

	Product 1	Product 2	Product 3
Alternative A	50,000 units	125,000 units	50,000 units
Alternative B	25,000 units	165,000 units	50,000 units
Alternative C	50,000 units	260,000 units	—
Alternative D	150,000 units	—	45,000 units
Alternative E	—	—	125,000 units

The results for the previous year are summarized below:

	Product 1 £	Product 1 £	Product 2 £	Product 2 £	Product 3 £	Product 3 £
Sales		350,000		625,000		675,000
Prime cost	150,000		250,000		350,000	
Variable o/head	75,000		125,000		150,000	
Fixed o/head	54,000		200,000		110,000	
		279,000		575,000		610,000
Profit		71,000		50,000		65,000
Sales in units		50,000		125,000		50,000

Assuming that no changes are envisaged which of the alternatives A to E would you recommend to management?

SOLUTION

Product 1	£	£
Sales 50,000 units		350,000
Variable costs		
Prime cost	150,000	
Variable o/head	75,000	
		225,000
TOTAL CONTRIBUTION		125,000

CONTRIBUTION PER UNIT SOLD $\dfrac{125,000}{50,000} = £2.50$

Product 2	£	£
Sales 125,000 units		625,000
Variable costs		
Prime cost	250,000	
Variable o/head	125,000	
		375,000
TOTAL CONTRIBUTION		250,000

CONTRIBUTION PER UNIT SOLD $\dfrac{250,000}{125,000} = £2$

Product 3	£	£
Sales 50,000 units		675,000
Variable costs		
Prime cost	350,000	
Variable o/head	150,000	
		500,000
TOTAL CONTRIBUTION		175,000

CONTRIBUTION PER UNIT $\dfrac{175,000}{50,000} = £3.50$

Applying these contributions to the available product mixes we arrive at the most profitable alternative as shown below and see that it is alternative C which gives a total contribution of £625,000. However, management may prefer option B as, although it makes a smaller contribution, it maintains all three of the products and could in the long run prove the better choice. Customers, on finding that they can no longer obtain product 3, may turn to other suppliers for all three of the products and management must decide whether to risk this by taking option C or minimizing the risk and choosing option B.

Contribution

Alternative

	Product 1	£	Product 2	£	Product 3	£	TOTAL £
A	50,000 units @ £2.50 =	125,000	125,000 units @ £2 =	250,000	50,000 units @ £3.50 =	175,000	550,000
B	25,000 units @ £2.50 =	62,500	165,000 units @ £2 =	330,000	50,000 units @ £3.50 =	175,000	567,500
C	50,000 units @ £2.50 =	125,000	250,000 units @ £2 =	500,000	—		625,000
D	150,000 units @ £2.50 =	375,000	—		45,000 units @ £3.50 =	157,500	532,500
E	—		—		125,000 units @ £3.50 =	437,500	437,500

QUESTION

11.1 An organization has undertaken some market research and the sales forecast is:

Sales at £10 each—10,000 units total value of sales £100,000
Sales at £9.50 each—15,000 units total value of sales £142,500
Sales at £9 each—20,000 units total value of sales £180,000
Sales at £8.50 each—25,000 units total value of sales £212,500

The costs of production are variable cost per unit £8 and annual fixed costs £10,000.

The company has the capacity to produce at any of the suggested levels but is at present selling 20,000 units at £9 each. Do you recommend any changes?

ANSWER

11.1

Units	Selling unit price	Variable cost	Contribution per unit	Total contribution
10,000	£10	£8	£2	£20,000
15,000	£9.50	£8	£1.50	£22,500
20,000	£9	£8	£1	£20,000
25,000	£8.50	£8	£0.50	£12,500

It seems that the greatest contribution is at 15,000 units, giving £22,500 and a profit of (£22,500 − 10,000), i.e., £12,500 provided customers are not upset by receiving smaller quantities than before. Good use can be made of the capacity that is released: 15,000 units should be produced and sold giving £2,500 more profit than at present.

TWELVE

DIFFERENTIAL COSTING
(Costing for decision making)

Marginal costing is applied over a period of time to a large number of problems. Differential costing applies the same techniques but accepts that each problem is unique and could well have different fixed costs over a period of time. In calculating departmental or product costs it is difficult to apportion those costs which bear no clear relationship to the products or departments concerned. Examples are proportion of managing director's salary, of rates or of finance costs to be charged.

The allocation of these costs can be made only on an arbitrary basis that is true for one set of conditions only; because of this, cost figures that have been prepared for one purpose should be closely examined before they are used for any other purpose. Differential costs are the costs that will be altered by a change in an organization's scale, mix, place or method of operating. The financial effect of any such change can be estimated only by distinguishing between the fixed costs, i.e., those that will be unaltered by the change, and the differential costs which are affected by the change. Differential costing is the term used to describe cost investigations which are set up to determine the effect of such changes.

Example A manager who runs his car 10,000 miles a year has worked out the costs to be:

	Pence per mile
Depreciation £1,000 p.a.	10.0
Maintenance £120 service every 5,000 miles	2.4
Maintenance £240 service every 10,000 miles	2.4
Tyres new set £200 every 20,000 miles	1.0
Licence and insurance £400 p.a.	4.0
Petrol and oil at 35 mpg	7.3
Annual interest on £12,000 car is £1,440	14.4
	41.5

He moves his job and has to travel 20 miles to his new place of employment, in addition to the normal 10,000 miles p.a. that he travels in his car. There is a bus that stops outside his front door and goes by the most direct route to his place of work. Bus and car are equally convenient. Which do you recommend he should use on financial grounds if the bus fare is £5 return per day?

SUGGESTED SOLUTION Using the differential costing approach the only additional costs of the car are servicing, tyres and fuel, the other costs are all fixed and have to be met. The car costs that are charged add up to:

	Pence per mile
5,000 mile service	2.4
10,000 mile service	2.4
Tyres	1.0
Fuel	7.3
	13.1

The costs for the bus are 40 miles at £5 = 12.5p per mile. On financial considerations alone the bus should be used.

Depreciation is normally charged on the age of an article rather than usage. However, it could be that heavy mileage would increase the annual cost of depreciation.

QUESTION

12.1 A product costs £9 when purchased from outside suppliers.
The annual production costs are:

	£
Salary of product manager	20,000
Depreciation of departmental machinery	6,000
Overhead from other departments allocated to the product	24,000
Variable overhead	30,000
Variable/prime/direct cost	60,000
TOTAL for 12,000 units	140,000

Cost per unit $\dfrac{140,000}{12,000}$ = £11.67. Working capital £15,000 at 12 per cent.

Do you recommend that the organization should buy in from the outside supplier or continue to produce the product itself?

ANSWER

12.1 In answering this question we have to decide which costs will be altered by stopping production and buying the product from outside suppliers. If this were done the savings would be prime cost £60,000, which is the cost of production in terms of materials and labour, and the variable overhead £30,000, which would largely be made up of power costs. It is assumed that the product manager would not be made redundant. The working capital would be released so that the interest of £1,800 would be saved.

The cost of buying from outside would be £9 plus the fixed costs of the department that would still have to be met which are:

	£
Product manager's salary	20,000
Depreciation of department machinery	6,000
Overhead allocated from other departments	24,000
	50,000

which is £4.17 per unit. This makes the cost of buying £13.17 per unit (£9 + £4.17) which is more than the production cost of £11.67+ interest on the working capital of 15p per unit (£11.82). In this case it is better to continue to manufacture ourselves.

If we assume that the plant manager is made redundant at no additional cost then the cost of buying in becomes:

	£
Depreciation of departmental machinery	6,000
Allocated overhead	24,000
	30,000

which is £2.50 per unit making the cost of buying £11.50. This is much closer to the production cost of £11.67 and changes the decision in that it is now apparently better to buy in the product than make it ourselves.

(2) The capital budgeting decision is extremely important to any organization because it generally involves incurring expenditure of large sums of money that will have an effect on the profitability of the organization for many years. The general budgeting process usually extends over ten years into the future and the capital budgeting process is part of this.

In all organizations the demand for funds for capital outlay exceeds the funds available, so some means of ranking these competing schemes has to be devised. Capital expenditure gives rise to fixed assets like land and buildings, plant and machinery and motor vehicles so the first step is to draw up a schedule of likely projects over the next ten years. This will be firm for the first and second years, flexible for the next three years, and tentative for the last five years.

One format for the capital budget may be:

SCHEME

	Yr 1 £'000s	Yr 2 £'000s	Yr 3 £'000s	Yr 4 £'000s	Yr 5 £'000s	Yr 6 £'000s	Yr 7 £'000s	Yr 8 £'000s	Yr 9 £'000s	Yr 10 £'000s
A	200	500	50	—	—	—	—	—	—	—
B	500	—	80	—	—	—	—	—	—	—
C	40	80	—	—	—	—	—	—	—	—
D	50	60	—	—	—	—	—	—	—	—
E	20	40	—	20	—	—	—	—	—	—
F	—	—	—	—	20	100	60	50	100	60
G	60	10	30	—	—	—	—	—	—	—
H	—	—	—	60	40	10	80	—	—	—
I	10	40	100	—	—	—	—	—	—	—
TOTAL	880	730	260	80	60	110	140	50	100	60

This will tell you how much money is likely to be required for capital purposes over the next ten years. The budget is not all-embracing, however, and if other schemes arise they cannot be excluded but must be considered. Having established the needs for the next 12 months a method has to be derived to rank the schemes. Some of them will of course select themselves on grounds of pure necessity. This may be brought about by a technological advance making some new equipment essential, or a breakdown making replacement necessary. There are many ways of ranking the remaining schemes but three will be described here that are in common usage. They are payback, return on investment, and net present value.

13.1 PAYBACK

Payback is frequently employed either alone or in conjunction with the net present value technique because managers are keen to know how quickly they are likely to recover their capital outlay. The sooner this can be achieved the better, so far as the organization is concerned, as the money is then available for other purposes. An example of a payback calculation would be if an organization were to consider installing a drink-dispensing machine in an office. The machine would cost £4,000 and be instrumental in generating an additional cash flow of £500 a year after the deduction of running costs. The payback would be eight years as it would take 4,000/500 = 8 years to recover the £4,000 capital outlay.

If the only criteria were financial and the organization was looking for a three-year payback the scheme would be rejected. If, on the other hand, a nine-year payback was required the scheme would be accepted *for further consideration*. It would not automatically go ahead but it would be grouped with the other schemes that met the payback criteria.

This basis is easy to understand and apply and recognizes that each £1 received earlier is more valuable than £1 received later, because the £1 received earlier can be invested at the going rate of interest which is denied to the person who receives the £1 later. However, it does not attempt to put a value on the £1 that is received earlier, neither does it consider the whole scheme. Cash flows generated after the payback period are completely ignored. Under this method all projects that meet the payback requirement go forward for further consideration and those that do not are rejected.

13.2 RETURN ON INVESTMENT

Under this method the average annual cash flow generated over the life of the asset is calculated and expressed as a percentage of the capital investment. This may be illustrated with the following example.

An organization is considering installing double glazing in its administrative offices. The cost is £40,000 and it is expected to result in savings on heating over the next 15 years of:

Year	£
1	1,000
2	2,200
3	2,500
4	2,600
5	2,800
6	3,000
7	3,200
8	3,200
9	3,200
10	3,300
11	3,300
12	3,400
13	3,400
14	3,500
15	3,500
Total	£44,100

$$\text{Average annual cash flow} = \frac{44,100 \ (\text{total})}{15 \ (\text{years})} = £2,940$$

This is expressed as a percentage of capital invested by multiplying

by 100 and dividing by the sum invested $\dfrac{2,940 \times 100}{40,000} = 7.35$ per cent

If the organization were looking for a 15 per cent return on the capital invested this scheme would not go forward for further consideration. On the other hand if a 6 per cent return was the criterion then it would receive further consideration.

This method of assessing capital investment schemes is easy to understand and does use the whole life of the scheme in arriving at a figure. Its major drawback is that it ignores the time value of money.

13.3 NET PRESENT VALUE

This is a discounted cash flow (DCF) approach to rank competing capital projects. It considers the whole life of the project and recognizes the time value of money. It is in common use, frequently in combination with the payback method. It may be illustrated by the following example.

There are two competing schemes, A and B, to produce a household good. Scheme A costs £80,000 to buy the necessary equipment which will last for eight years. The equipment is sophisticated and results in savings in material and labour over the eight years of:

Year	Savings (£)
1	9,000
2	18,000
3	20,000
4	20,000
5	20,000
6	15,000
7	10,000
8	4,000

Scheme B requires a capital investment of £60,000 on not such sophisticated equipment which will also last for eight years. It is expected to generate the following savings over its life:

Year	Savings (£)
1	6,000
2	9,000
3	10,000
4	10,000
5	10,000
6	9,000
7	5,000
8	5,000

Which of the two schemes should be chosen?

Scheme A costs £80,000. This is now, so the value of the money is now. Savings assume that they are achieved at the end of the year in question and the organization could invest money at 11 per cent. This means that the cost of capital is 11 per cent, and any schemes introduced must be instrumental in earning or saving more than this. Tables are prepared to show how time affects the value of money and a set is included in this book on pages 187 to 194. In this case we will have to use the 11 per cent table.

Year		£	Factor	Present value £
0	Outlay			80,000
1	Savings	9,000	× 0.9009	8,108
2		18,000	× 0.8116	14,609
3		20,000	× 0.7312	14,624
4		20,000	× 0.6587	13,174
5		20,000	× 0.5935	11,870
6		15,000	× 0.5346	8,019
7		10,000	× 0.4817	4,817
8		4,000	× 0.4339	1,736
	PRESENT VALUE			76,957
	NET PRESENT VALUE			− 3,043

This tells us that the present value of all the future savings brought about by scheme A is £76,957 when the cost of capital is 11 per cent. This, when compared with the capital outlay of £80,000, gives a negative net present value (NPV) of £3,044 which would mean that the scheme would not be further considered as the 11 per cent criterion has not been met. The table used was the 11 per cent table under the third column title of 'Present value of £1'. From this you see that if you could invest money at 11 per cent, a pound received in ten years' time would be worth only 35p when compared with a pound that you hold now.

Using the same procedures for scheme B we have:

Year		£	Factor	Present value £
0	Outlay			60,000
1	Savings	6,000	× 0.9009	5,405
2		9,000	× 0.8116	7,304
3		10,000	× 0.7312	7,312
4		10,000	× 0.6587	6,587
5		10,000	× 0.5935	5,935
6		9,000	× 0.5346	4,811
7		5,000	× 0.4817	2,409
8		5,000	× 0.4339	2,170
	PRESENT VALUE			41,933
	NET PRESENT VALUE			− 18,067

Neither of these schemes would be accepted using the 11 per cent criterion, but if it was essential that one was chosen then scheme A is the better of the two since it has a NPV of −£3,043 compared with B which gives NPV of − £18,067.

An alternative approach to decide which of these two schemes should be chosen, if it had already been decided that one of them was essential, would be to use the differential approach:

£

Additional cost of scheme A now (£80,000 − £60,000) 20,000

Additional savings generated by scheme A:

Year 1 (£9,000 − £6,000) £3,000 × 0.9009		2,703
2 (£18,000 − £9,000) £9,000 × 0.8116		7,304
3 (£20,000 − £10,000) £10,000 × 0.7312		7,312
4 (£20,000 − £10,000) £10,000 × 0.6587		6,587
5 (£20,000 − £10,000) £10,000 × 0.5935		5,935
6 (£15,000 − £9,000) £6,000 × 0.5346		3,208
7 (£10,000 − £5,000) £5,000 × 0.4817		2,408
8 (£4,000 − £5,000) − £1,000 × 0.4339		(434)

PRESENT VALUE   35,023

NET PRESENT VALUE   + 15,023

This shows that the extra savings generated by scheme A, discounted to their present value, exceed the additional cost of scheme A by £15,023 and that, all other things being equal, scheme A would be chosen.

The capital budgeting process is essential and some method of choosing between competing schemes must be used that is seen to be fair. If this is not done unrest will be fermented, as the dominant character or department in the organization will always obtain a lion's share of the monetary cake, which will often not be deserved. Even in the best run organizations the unexpected happens, like a technological advance making equipment obsolete or machinery breaking down. In these cases capital expenditure has to be incurred from pure necessity, but it does not mean that the capital budget should not be prepared, nor does it imply that it should be completely ignored.

Internal rate of return

A second discounted cash flow approach to the ranking of competing capital projects is the internal rate of return. Like NPV it considers the whole life of the project, recognizes the time value of money, and is in common use, frequently in combination with the payback method. It will generally lead to the same decisions as are reached when the net present value approach is employed. This method requires the interest rate that will make the total of the future cash flows exactly equal to the original investment. This concept may be illustrated by returning to our example of two competing schemes on page 101.

Scheme A

Try 11%

Year			Factor	Present value £	Present value £
		£			
0	Costs	80,000 × 1			80,000
1	Savings	9,000 × 0.9009		8,108	
2		18,000 × 0.8116		14,609	
3		20,000 × 0.7312		14,624	
4		20,000 × 0.6587		13,174	
5		20,000 × 0.5935		11,870	
6		15,000 × 0.5346		8,019	
7		10,000 × 0.4817		4,817	
8		4,000 × 0.4339		1,736	

PRESENT VALUE   76,957

NET PRESENT VALUE   − 3,043

This has a negative NPV so we try to find an interest rate that will give a positive NPV and, by interpolation, arrive at the interest rate that gives a NPV of zero (0). That will be the internal rate of return (IRR). As 11 per cent gives a negative NPV, anything above 11 per cent will increase the size of the negative NPV as it will reduce further the present value of the future cash flows. It is therefore, necessary to try a percentage below 11 per cent.

Scheme A

Try 7%

Year			Factor	Present value £	Present value £
		£			
0	Costs	80,000 × 1			80,000
1	Savings	9,000 × 0.9346		8,411	
2		18,000 × 0.8734		15,721	
3		20,000 × 0.8163		16,326	
4		20,000 × 0.7629		15,258	
5		20,000 × 0.7130		14,260	
6		15,000 × 0.6663		9,994	
7		10,000 × 0.6227		6,227	
8		4,000 × 0.5820		2,328	

PRESENT VALUE   88,525

NET PRESENT VALUE   + 8,525

We now have both a negative and a positive NPV and can arrive at the IRR by interpolation.

$$\text{Positive NPV\%} + \text{positive and negative NPV\%} \left(\frac{\text{Positive NPV}}{\text{sum of NPVs, ignoring signs}} \right)$$

$$7\% + 4\% \left(\frac{8{,}525}{11{,}568} \right) = 7\% + (4 \times 0.74) = 7\% + 2.96 = \sim 10\%$$

We can test this by trying 10 per cent and seeing how close the result is to zero. You will have noticed that in the calculation of the IRR the 7 per cent is the percentage that gave a positive NPV, the 4 per cent is the difference between the 7 per cent and the 11 per cent which gave the negative NPV, the numerator is the positive NPV of £8,525 at 7 per cent, while the denominator is the addition of the two NPVs ignoring their signs; that is (£3,044 + £8,525) = £11,569.

Test

Try 10%

Year		£	Factor	Present value £	Present value £
0	Costs	80,000 × 1			80,000
1	Savings	9,000 × 0.9091		8,182	
2		18,000 × 0.8264		14,875	
3		20,000 × 0.7513		15,026	
4		20,000 × 0.6830		13,660	
5		20,000 × 0.6209		12,418	
6		15,000 × 0.5645		8,467	
7		10,000 × 0.5132		5,132	
8		4,000 × 0.4665		1,866	
		PRESENT VALUE			79,626
		NET PRESENT VALUE			− 374

This test confirms that interpolation has enabled us to arrive at the IRR which is 10 per cent. The slight difference of £374 can be accounted for by rounding up to 10 per cent the 9.96 per cent that the calculation gave.

The cost of funds is 11 per cent, that is the *opportunity cost* of the investment, and the return is 10 per cent so the scheme would not be considered any further. This agrees with the decision reached when the NPV method is used. Using the same approach for scheme B we have:

Scheme B

Try 11%

Year		Factor £	Present value £	Present value £
0	Costs	60,000 × 1		60,000
1	Savings	6,000 × 0.9009	5,405	
2		9,000 × 0.8116	7,304	
3		10,000 × 0.7312	7,312	
4		10,000 × 0.6587	6,587	
5		10,000 × 0.5935	5,935	
6		9,000 × 0.5346	4,811	
7		5,000 × 0.4817	2,409	
8		5,000 × 0.4339	2,170	
		PRESENT VALUE		41,933
		NET PRESENT VALUE		− 18,067

The negative NPV means that we have to look for a lower rate of interest that gives a positive result and then arrive at the IRR by interpolation. Try 3 per cent.

Scheme B

Try 3%

Year		Factor £	Present value £	Present value £
0	Costs	60,000 × 1		60,000
1	Savings	6,000 × 0.9709	5,825	
2		9,000 × 0.9426	8,483	
3		10,000 × 0.9151	9,151	
4		10,000 × 0.8885	8,885	
5		10,000 × 0.8626	8,626	
6		9,000 × 0.8375	7,538	
7		5,000 × 0.8131	4,066	
8		5,000 × 0.7894	3,947	
		PRESENT VALUE		56,521
		NET PRESENT VALUE		− 3,479

This is a negative NPV so we try 1 per cent.

Scheme B

Try 1%

Year		£	Factor	Present value £	Present value £
0	Costs	60,000 × 1			60,000
1	Savings	6,000 × 0.9901		5,941	
2		9,000 × 0.9803		8,823	
3		10,000 × 0.9706		9,706	
4		10,000 × 0.9610		9,610	
5		10,000 × 0.9515		9,515	
6		9,000 × 0.9420		8,478	
7		5,000 × 0.9327		4.664	
8		5,000 × 0.9235		4,618	

PRESENT VALUE 61,355

NET PRESENT VALUE + 1,355

This gives a positive NPV and by interpolation the IRR may be found.

$$1\% + 2\% \left(\frac{1,355}{4,834}\right) = 1\% + (2 \times 0.28) = 1\% + 0.56 \sim 1\%$$

This scheme would be rejected, as it was using the NPV approach, where the 11 per cent criterion is imposed, but if it was essential that one was chosen it would be scheme A as it gives the higher return of 10 per cent as opposed to 1 per cent for scheme B.

CAPITAL INVESTMENT DECISIONS QUESTIONS

13.1 Overfull has a problem with space that is expected to last for seven years. A cheap pre-fabricated building is available that will last seven years and be removed after that time. Enquiries reveal that heating costs will be £10,000 p.a. This seems rather high and the question of heating is investigated further. Heat loss from this type of building is very great. If insulation was carried out for £24,000, the heating costs would be reduced to £5,000.

Overfull's cost of capital is 9 per cent. State whether the building should be insulated.

13.2 Suppliers are making a special component and require a new machine. It is available in the standard model which costs £15,000, lasts five years and has a scrap value of £2,000. The raw material costs will be £10,000 a year.

A more advanced model costs £30,000, lasts five years and has a scrap value of £4,000. Its greater efficiency will reduce raw material costs to £6,000 a year. If all other costs will be the same and supplier's cost of capital is 14 per cent which machine should be purchased?

Suggested Answers
13.1

	Year	£ Factor	£
Cost of insulation	0	24,000 × 1	24,000
Savings	1	5,000 × 0.9174	4,587
	2	5,000 × 0.8417	4,209
	3	5,000 × 0.7722	3,861
	4	5,000 × 0.7084	3,542
	5	5,000 × 0.6499	3,249
	6	5,000 × 0.5963	2,982
	7	5,000 × 0.5470	2,735

PRESENT VALUE	25,165
NET PRESENT VALUE (NPV)	+ 1,165

The discounted savings exceed the cost of insulation so it is worth going ahead and insulating the building.

An alternative approach that can be employed when the same sum of money is involved over a number of years is to use the cumulative table under column 4 (see Table A, pages 187–194, if the savings occur at the year end, or column 5, 'Present value of £1 received continuously', if the savings or cash inflow are continuous throughout the period. In this example the calculation will then become:

£

Cost of insulation	24,000
Savings using column 4 and year 7 of present value tables	
£5,000 × 5.0330 PRESENT VALUE	25,165
NET PRESENT VALUE	+ 1,165

Using column 5 and year 7 we have

£

Cost of insulation	24,000
Savings £5,000 × 5.2562 PRESENT VALUE	26,281
NET PRESENT VALUE	+ 2,281

In this example we have a greater NPV because the savings are achieved right throughout each year rather than waiting until the year end.

To use the IRR approach we start from the position of a positive NPV of £1,165 when 9 per cent is applied as the cost of capital as calculated above. To obtain a negative NPV a greater cost of capital must be used.

Try 12%		*Factor*	*Present value*	*Present value*
Year				
		£	£	£
0	Costs	24,000 × 1		24,000
1	Savings	5,000 × 0.8929	4,465	
2		5,000 × 0.7979	3,989	
3		5,000 × 0.7118	3,559	
4		5,000 × 0.6355	3,178	
5		5,000 × 0.5674	2,837	
6		5,000 × 0.5066	2,533	
7		5,000 × 0.4523	2,261	

PRESENT VALUE   22,822

NET PRESENT VALUE   − 1,178

Using interpolation to find the IRR we have

$$9\% + 3\% \left(\frac{1,165}{2,343}\right) = 9\% + (3 \times 0.49) = 9\% + 1.47 \sim 10\%$$

This gives an IRR of approximately 10 per cent which is greater than the required 9 per cent so the insulation would be carried out.

£

13.2 Year 0 additional cost of the advanced machine
   (£30,000 − £15,000)   15,000

Savings obtained:
  Raw material costs reduced from £10,000
     to £6,000 a year for five years
  £4,000 × 3.4331   13,732
  Additional scrap year 5, £2,000 × 0.5194   1,039

PRESENT VALUE   14,771

NET PRESENT VALUE   − 229

The discounted savings engendered by the more expensive machine are less than its additional cost so it is better to buy the cheaper machine. However, it is a marginal decision as the difference is only £229.

If the continuous table is used we have:

		£
£4,000 × 3.6682		14,672
£2,000 × 0.5194		1,039
	PRESENT VALUE	15,711
	NET PRESENT VALUE	+ 711

This gives a positive NPV and reverses the decision, which highlights the fact that the basis on which the estimates are being made must be clearly understood. In this case the decision will probably be based on personal preference.

The solution to the question using the IRR approach becomes

Advanced model using 13 per cent

Year		Factor £	Present value £	Present value £
0	Additional outlay	15,000 × 1		15,000
1–5	Savings	4,000 × 3.5172	14,069	
5	Additional scrap	2,000 × 0.5428	1,086	
	PRESENT VALUE			15,155
	NET PRESENT VALUE			+ 155

There is a negative NPV when 14 per cent is employed as calculated previously so we can see at a glance that the IRR is going to be around 14 per cent. Using interpolation we have

$$13\% + 1\% \left(\frac{155}{384}\right) = 13\% + (1 \times 0.4) = 13\% + 1.4 = 14.4\%$$

This gives an IRR of approximately 14 per cent which our previous calculations indicated it would be. It becomes a marginal decision whether to buy the advanced or standard machine and will be made on grounds of personal preference.

The capital budgeting techniques are available to all managers but they are unfortunately all too often ignored. The vast majority of capital investment decisions are in my experience made on the basis of urgency, that is, money having to be spent to enable the organization to survive. This does not obviate the need for capital budget programmes, but it does mean that they very often have to undergo major adjustments, which is to be expected of any system of forecasting in conditions of uncertainty.

NOTE TO CHAPTER 13: RELATIONSHIP BETWEEN DISCOUNTING AND COMPOUNDING

The tables used to calculate the present value work in the opposite direction to those used to calculate compound interest, which gives the future value of a sum regularly invested. These sets of tables, that are commonly employed in compounding and discounting calculations, are derived from the same basic mathematical formula which, using the notation given, becomes

Let a sum P be invested at time 0
Let a sum P be invested at the end of each subsequent period, i.e., at time 1, 2, etc.
Let the interest rate per period be i (a fraction)
Let the number of periods be n
Let the value at any time be S

1. S_1 the value of the initial capital sum P

End of period

1	$P + iP = P(1 + i)$
2	$P(1 + i) + iP(1 + i) = P(1 + i)^2$

. . . .

n	$P(1 + i)^n$

2. S_2 the value of the regular investments P

End of period

1	P
2	$P(1 + i) + P$
3	$[P(1 + i) + P][(1 + i)] + P = P(1 + i)^2 + (1 + i) + 1$
4	$P[(1 + i)^3 + (1 + i)^2 + (1 + i) + 1]$
n	$S_2 = P[(1 + i)^{n-1} + (1 + i)^{n-2} + ... (1 + i)^2 + (1 + i) + 1]$

$$...(1 + i)S_2 = P[(1 + i)^n + (1 + i)^{n-1} + ...(1 + i)^3 + (1 + i)^2 + (1 + i)]$$
$$...(1 + i)S_2 - S_2 = P[(1 + i)^n - 1]$$

and hence
$$S_2 = \frac{P[(1 + i)^n - 1]}{i}$$

Thus the total value at the end of period n is S

$$S = S_1 + S_2 = P(1 + i)^n + P\frac{[(1 + i)^n - 1]}{i}$$

The formula can be used in different ways according to the values given and the calculation to be performed. That for discounting, where a single amount is involved, is

$$P = \frac{S}{(1 + i)^n}$$

and for compounding

$$S = P(1 + i)^n$$

Where uniform payments are concerned the formula for discounting is

$$P = - \left[\frac{(1 + i)^n - 1}{i(1 + i)^n} \right] P$$

and for compounding

$$S = P \frac{[(1 + i)^n - 1]}{i}$$

CHAPTER

FOURTEEN

RAISING PERMANENT AND LONG-TERM FINANCE

Sources from which finance may be raised have been discussed in Chapters 1 and 2 but the processes by which it can be raised were not considered. The purpose of this chapter is to explore the ways in which permanent and long-term capital or money may be raised. Permanent capital is provided by the owners of the business either by introducing money from their own resources or by retaining profits in the business instead of distributing them as dividends. The retained profits are shown as reserves in the balance sheet. Long-term capital is obtained by borrowing money that will have to be repaid at some time in the future. The borrowing may be from either individuals, financial institutions or others with money to invest like the various pension funds. We will now investigate each of these types of capital in turn.

14.1 PERMANENT CAPITAL

Permanent capital can be raised by the issue of shares either 'ordinary' or 'preference'. Ordinary shares carry voting rights and enable the shareholders to vote on matters of importance affecting the business. The ordinary shareholders are the owners of the business and appoint directors to act on their behalf in running the business. The directors having been appointed by the ordinary shareholders could in theory be removed by them. In practice this is extremely difficult to achieve and rarely happens. This is because the directors themselves hold large number of shares. You should view with suspicion any organization whose directors hold few or no shares. It means that the directors do not believe in the organization that they are running, and if they have no faith in it why should the general investor?

Each ordinary share carries a voting right so that the more shares you own the greater your say in what should be done. Anyone who owns more than 50 per cent of the ordinary share capital normally controls the business. The ordinary shareholders are the equity holders. They take the biggest risk and can, if things go badly, as with Polly Peck, lose virtually everything. Consequently when things go well, they expect the biggest return in terms of income by way of dividend received and capital growth through an increase in the market price of a share. The capital is permanent because the business is under no obligation to buy back the shares that it has sold. If a shareholder wishes to recover the money that has been invested in shares then he or she has to do so by selling the shares to a purchaser through the mechanism of the Stock Exchange. If the share price has risen more

113

will be obtained for the shares than was originally invested in them and a capital gain realized. On the other hand, if the price has fallen less will be obtained than was originally paid and a loss incurred. The dividend paid to the ordinary shareholders is at the discretion of the directors but it will not normally vary much from year to year. It has to be paid out of after tax profits but may be paid out of previously unused profits if the directors so decide. If at all possible directors will maintain dividends and not withhold them. It is interesting to note that in the difficult climate of 1991 many organizations are asking shareholders if they would like to receive their dividends in the form of additional shares instead of money; and some are even talking of withholding the dividend altogether.

Preference shares generally carry no voting rights and as the name implies holders receive their dividends before the ordinary shareholders. The rate of dividend is stated on the face of the share, e.g., 9 per cent preference share. The 9 per cent is based on the nominal value of the share and not on the profits earned or the market value of the share. The nominal value of any share is shown on the face of the share certificate and it is normally 25p. There are other nominal values and 50p and £1 are often seen. The nominal value is employed to show the value of the issued share capital in the balance sheet. Shares are usually issued for more than the nominal value and the difference between the nominal value and the amount actually received is shown in the share premium account under reserves.

Example   If a company issues

10,000 ordinary shares of 25p for £1 and
5,000 9% preference shares of 25p for 50p the balance sheet will show:

	£
Issued share capital	
10,000 ordinary shares	2,500
5,000 9% preference shares	1,250
Reserves	
Share premium account	8,750
The total amount raised is	
10,000 × £1 =	10,000
+ 5,000 × 50p =	2,500
	———
	12,500

but only £3,750 of this is shown in the issued share capital section. The balance of £8,750 is shown under reserves as share premium account. In practice shares would not normally be issued to raise such small sums of money. The smallest amount raised by a general issue of shares would usually be £500,000.

The preference shareholders receive their dividend before the ordinary shareholders and if the company fails they are paid what is due to them before the ordinary shareholders receive anything. The risk is smaller than that of the ordinary shareholders and because of this the ordinary shareholders expect a bigger dividend and a greater capital gain than the preference shareholders if things go well. In other respects the ordinary and preference shareholders are treated in the same way.

There are four ways in which ordinary shares are normally issued but only two of these result in additional finance for the issuing company.

(a) Capitalization issue (also known as a 'scrip', 'free' or 'bonus' issue).
(b) Rights issue.
(c) Vendor consideration.
(d) Placing.

Capitalization issue

The purpose of a capitalization issue is to bring the issued capital into closer relationship with the capital employed in a business. It raises no additional money for the business and no money changes hands. Shares are normally issued to the existing shareholders in proportion to their existing holdings by capitalizing reserves. This reduces the reserves and increases the number of ordinary shares in issue which makes the market value of each ordinary share fall. Each individual shareholder is no better or worse off than he/she was previously because the additional shares have gone to existing shareholders. A person who previously had one share with a market value of £3 may now have three shares each of which has a market value of £1.

The relevant section of a business's balance sheet before and after a capitalization issue may be illustrated as follows:

	£
Issued share capital	
100,000 ordinary shares	25,000
Reserves	
Share premium account	175,000
Profit and loss account	100,000

After capitalization of £100,000 of the reserves by the issue of 400,000 25p shares

	£
Issued share capital	
500,000 ordinary shares	125,000
Reserves	
Share premium account	75,000
Profit and loss account	100,000

The total of the issued share capital and reserves remains at £300,000 but it has been adjusted to bring the issued share capital into a closer relationship with the capital employed in the business.

Rights issue

The purpose of a rights issue is to raise additional finance to allow a business to expand or prepare for a more competitive market situation. A rights issue is normally made at a price which is below the current market value of the shares. If it were not there would be no incentive for the existing shareholders to take up the offer. It cannot be made below the nominal value of the shares less a maximum commission of 10 per cent. The shares must be offered to the existing shareholders first because if they were offered to the public at large there would be a dilution of the existing holders' rights and benefits. In view of this a company in making a new issue of ordinary shares for cash must allot such rights to existing holders if its shares are quoted on the Stock Exchange. The term *rights* issue refers to the rights of the existing shareholders to maintain their relationship with the business.

When a rights issue takes place the issued share capital of the business and the bank balance will both increase as will the reserves if the issue is made at above the par value. This may be illustrated using the following balance sheet.

	£'000s	£'000s
Fixed assets:		
Land and buildings		400
Plant and machinery		100
Fixtures and fittings		50
		550
Current assets:		
Stock	60	
Debtors	10	
Bank	5	
	75	
Deduct		
Current liabilities	65	
Working capital		10
Net capital employed		560
Financed by		
Issued share capital		
1,800,000 ordinary shares		450
Reserves		
Share premium account		80
Profit and loss account		30
		560

If the business now makes a rights issue of one new share for every nine shares already held then an additional 200,000

$$\left(\frac{1,800,000}{9}\right)$$

shares will be issued and the issued share capital will become £500,000 (£450,000 + £50,000). Issuing the shares for £1, which is above their nominal value of 25p and below their assumed current market value of £1.30p, will have a twofold effect. Firstly, the share premium account will be increased by £150,000 (200,000 × £0.75) to £230,000 (£80,000 + £150,000) and, secondly, the bank balance will be increased by £200,000 to £205,000 (£5,000 + £200,000). The discount of 30p between the current market value of £1.30 and the issue price of £1 would help to ensure that the rights issue was taken up.

Placings will only normally be allowed in the following circumstances:

(a) Where existing shareholders wish to dispose of shares which they have because of a rights issue or a vendor consideration issue (vendor consideration will be discussed next).
(b) Where ordinary shares in a company not previously listed on the Stock Exchange are to be issued.
(c) Where an already listed business wishes to issue additional shares. If the existing shareholders object this can only be done by way of a rights issue.

The effect on the balance sheet of issuing shares by means of a placing is the same as that for a rights issue which was previously illustrated.

Vendor consideration

The purpose of the issue of vendor consideration shares is to enable one business to acquire another business purely by issuing shares. It enables the acquiring business to keep its cash resources intact while at the same time giving the acquired business the opportunity to raise money by selling some of the shares it has been given. Where a part equity – part cash settlement is required by the vendor it is achieved by splitting the shares issued into two parts. The first comprises those shares the vendors intend to retain. The second comprises those shares that will later be sold by vendors for cash in the market place. The business issuing the shares does not receive any cash at all. The effect on the balance sheet will be for the issued share capital and reserves to increase and for a subsidiary company of the same value to appear amongst the fixed assets. This may be illustrated using the previous balance sheet and assuming the purchase is achieved by issuing 200,000 25p shares for £1, as follows:

	£'000s	£'000s
Fixed assets:		
Land and buildings		400
Plant and machinery		100
Fixtures and fittings		50
Investment in subsidiary company		200
		750
Current assets:		
Stocks	60	
Debtors	10	
Bank	5	
	75	
Deduct		
Current liabilities	65	
Working capital		10
Net capital employed		760
Financed by:		
Issued share capital		
2,000,000 ordinary shares		500
Reserves		
Share premium account		230
Profit and loss account		30
		760

The following example, using Green Designs plc, further illustrates the effects of issuing vendor consideration shares.

Green Designs plc
Balance sheet as at 30 November 1992

	£'000s	£'000s
Fixed Assets:		
Land and buildings		400
Plant and machinery		150
Fixtures and fittings		80
Motor vehicles		20
		650
Current assets:		
Stocks	100	
Debtors	80	
Bank	30	
	210	
Deduct		
Current liabilities	180	
Working capital		30
Net capital employed		680
Financed by:		
Issued share capital		
2,000,000 ordinary shares		500
Reserves		
Share premium account		100
Profit and loss account		80
		680

If another business is purchased for £300,000 by using 100,000 vendor consideration shares at £3 each then the balance sheet will be altered in three respects. The issued share capital becomes 2,100,000 ordinary shares valued at £525,000 (£500,000 + (100,000 × 25p). The share premium £375,000 (£100,000 + (100,000 × £2.75p)). The fixed assets increased by £300,000, being the value of the subsidiary business acquired, and the balance sheet will become:

Green Designs plc
Balance sheet as at 30 November 1992

	£'000s	£'000s
Fixed Assets:		
Land and buildings		400
Plant and machinery		150
Fixtures and fittings		80
Motor vehicles		20
Subsidiary undertaking		300
		950
Current assets:		
Stocks	100	
Debtors	80	
Bank	30	
	210	
Deduct		
Current liabilities	180	
Working capital		30
Net capital employed		980
Financed by:		
Issued share capital		
2,100,000 ordinary shares		525
Reserves		
Share premium account		375
Profit and loss account		80
		980

Placing

The purpose of a placing is to raise money for a business as cheaply as possible. It is only allowed where there is unlikely to be significant public demand for the shares and is usually restricted to £1.5m value of shares at the placing price. The placing involves the sale of shares by an issuing house or broker through the market to their own clients. The advantages of placings are that they are relatively cheap to effect because they avoid much of the marketing and administrative expense usually incurred and that the shares can be quickly and efficiently sold.

The permanent capital of a business comes only through the owners either directly by means of new money that they invest or indirectly through profits that they allow to remain in the business. The methods by which it is raised do differ however as we have seen in this chapter.

14.2 LONG-TERM CAPITAL

Long-term capital can be raised by borrowing from the money market but the amount is restricted by the Articles of Association of the business. The borrowing will also be affected by the market's perception of the management and its record over recent years. A successful business will find it easier to borrow and obtain a lower rate of interest than a badly managed organization. Long-term loans are normally obtained through the issue of debentures in £100 stock units. The debenture is a piece of paper which states the number of £100 units and the dates over which it may be repaid. The holder of debenture, or loan stock as it is sometimes called, is a creditor of the company and has a right to an annual return, regardless of whether or not profits are made, with the promise of the repayment of a fixed sum of money by a set date in the future.

Debentures may be secured or unsecured but unsecured loan stock can only be raised by large safe companies like ICI or IBM. It carries a rate of interest of about ½ per cent higher than that for a secured debenture. Secured debentures have either a floating charge or a fixed charge on the assets of the borrowing organization. An example of a fixed charge would be a debenture which is issued against the security of the buildings. Such a debenture is called a mortgage debenture and gives the lender the right to sell the buildings and recover the amount loaned should the business default on payment of interest or fail to repay the principal by the due date. A floating charge does not relate to any specific asset but 'floats' over all the assets until such time as the business defaults. Should this happen the charge would cease to float and descend on the assets so that they could only be sold in order to repay the debenture holders.

The debenture stock may be issued at par, that is, £100 cash for each £100 stock or at slightly below par, which is a way of manipulating the effective rate of interest payable and making the stock more attractive to lenders. If, for example, it is issued at £100 with a rate of interest of 11 per cent then the rate is obviously 11 per cent. If however it is issued at £95 this means that every £95 invested will secure £100 worth of stock and the interest rate becomes 11.58 per cent. Not only this but when the loan is redeemed the lender will receive £100 for each £95 invested.

The debenture can normally be redeemed during any one of a number of years at the discretion of the borrower. This increases the possibility that the business will be able to obtain the money necessary to repay the loan on reasonable terms. Most businesses do not generate sufficient cash from their own activities to repay the borrowings as they fall due. They either issue additional shares or take fresh borrowings, and a spread of dates on which this can be done enables the directors to choose a favourable time to do so. The effect on the balance sheet of raising long-term capital by the issue of debentures would be for the bank balance to increase amongst the current assets and for the long-term liabilities to also increase. This may be illustrated using the following example. A debenture loan of £200,000 is raised with a 11 per cent debenture redeemable 2010–2014 which will result in the original balance sheet of Green Designs plc becoming:

	£'000s	£'000s
Fixed assets:		
Land and buildings		400
Plant and machinery		150
Fixtures and fittings		80
Motor vehicles		20
		650
Current assets:		
Stocks	100	
Debtors	80	
Bank	230	
	410	
Less Current liabilities	180	
Working capital		230
Net capital employed		880
Financed by:		
Issued share capital		
2,000,000 ordinary shares		500
Reserves		
Share premium account		100
Profit and loss account		80
Long-term liability		
(Creditors repayable after more than one year)		
11% Debenture		200
		880

The money would not of course remain in the bank for very long but would be employed in the purchase of new fixed assets or in other ways to enable the business to run more effectively.

Whenever businesses need finance managers have to carefully consider whether it should be long term or permanent, and always have to bear in mind prevailing market conditions.

FIFTEEN

GEARING—COST OF CAPITAL

There are two points of view about the way in which an organization obtains its money and the cost of that money. The traditional approach is that there is a relationship between equity moneys and borrowed moneys at which the weighted average cost of capital will be minimized. Modigliani and Miller put forward the idea that in the long term the cost of raising money would be the same, whether through borrowed moneys or equity moneys raised by the issue of shares. The gearing of an organization is the relationship between share capital and borrowed funds; as borrowings increase the gearing is raised. No empirical evidence has yet been found to support the Modigliani and Miller approach so that the traditional view will be taken for the rest of this chapter.

Under the traditional view the weighted average cost of capital may be said to vary in relation to the gearing of the organization as shown in Figure 15.1.

This indicates that the way in which an organization obtains its capital is important and financial managers should strive to obtain the level of gearing that minimizes the weighted cost of capital. Equity holders take the greatest risk, in that if the business fails they are the

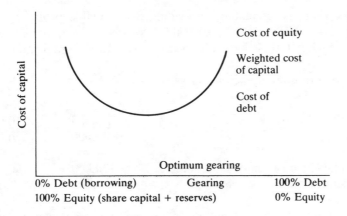

Figure 15.1 Cost of Capital Graph

last to be paid and if profits are low they will receive little or no dividend. In view of this they look for a high return on their investment by way of dividends. Lenders are normally secured so that if the business fails they will recover their money; interest is a business expense that has to be paid whether or not profit is being generated, unlike dividends which can only be paid out of profits. This means that lenders are satisfied with a lower return than shareholders as they perceive that they are taking a smaller risk. This holds good as borrowing increases so far as the lenders are concerned, but the equity holders require larger and larger returns as they see the risk that they will receive no dividends increase. The borrowing will reach a point at which lenders believe that there is a risk that interest payments may not be met in full and so demand a higher return on their loans. At this point the cost of borrowing and the weighted average cost of capital will both start to increase. The problem facing financial managers is to know this point and to endeavour to achieve it.

The impact of gearing on the profits that are available to the ordinary shareholders can best be illustrated as follows:

	Company A £	Company B £
Share capital £1 ordinary shares	1,000,000	700,000
Loan 10% debenture	400,000	700,000
Net capital employed	1,400,000	1,400,000

The two companies are employing the same net capital but Company A has relatively low gearing and Company B is relatively highly geared. Suppose now they each made the same profit of £70,000 before interest:

	£	£
Profit	70,000	70,000
Interest	40,000	70,000
Available for ordinary shareholders	30,000	NIL
Possible dividend per share	3p	NIL

The dividend per share is calculated by dividing the available profits by the number of shares issued. In this case it is £30,000 ÷ 1,000,000 shares giving 3p per share. When profits are low there is a high risk that shareholders in highly geared organizations will receive no dividend.

If the profit before interest increases to £210,000 we have:

	£	£
Profit	210,000	210,000
Interest	40,000	70,000
Available for ordinary shareholders	170,000	140,000
Possible dividend per share	17p	20p

When profits are high, shareholders in highly geared organizations receive greater dividends because there are fewer shares to receive dividends. Dividends have an effect on share prices so those of highly geared organizations fluctuate more widely than those of less highly geared businesses. Generally, investors do not like too great a fluctuation in either earnings per share or share prices, unless they are always upwards, so financial managers aim to obtain satisfactory gearing. Another reason is that if you borrow so much that you cannot afford the interest payments you will go out of business altogether. A recent example of this was Coloroll.

The effect of gearing on the weighted average of capital of an organization may be illustrated by the following example of two organizations that employ the same net capital but have different structures

Source of capital	£	Proportion of total capital %	Cost of capital %	Weighted cost of capital %
A Company				
Ordinary shares	2,000,000	41.7	12	5.00
12% Preference shares	1,000,000	20.8	12	2.50
Reserves	1,500,000	31.3	12	3.76
10% Debentures	300,000	6.2	10	0.62
	4,800,000	100.0		11.88
B Company				
Ordinary shares	1,500,000	31.3	12	3.76
12% Preference shares	1,000,000	20.8	12	2.50
Reserves	300,000	6.2	12	0.74
10% Debentures	2,000,000	41.7	10	4.17
	4,800,000	100.0		11.17

It can be seen that B Company, the more highly geared, has a lower weighted average cost of capital than A Company; 11.17 per cent as opposed to 11.88 per cent. This may not seem much but it ignores the impact of corporation tax. Interest on debenture loans is charged to profits before the liability to corporation tax is computed. Therefore, it reduces the corporation tax payable by the organization while the other sources of capital have no impact on corporation tax. If we assume that both Companies A and B are paying corporation tax at 50 per cent, then the cost of the loans to the organization (in terms of the net impact on profits) is not the 10 per cent payable to the lenders but only 5 per cent because of the tax allowance. The comparison between the two companies then becomes:

Source of capital	£	Proportion of total capital %	Cost of capital %	Weighted cost of capital %
A Company				
Ordinary shares	2,000,000	41.7	12	5.00
12% Preference shares	1,000,000	20.8	12	2.50
Reserves	1,500,000	31.3	12	3.75
10% Debentures	300,000	6.2	5	0.31
	4,800,000	100.0		11.56
	£	%	%	%
B Company				
Ordinary shares	1,500,000	31.3	12	3.76
12% Preference shares	1,000,000	20.8	12	2.50
Reserves	300,000	6.2	12	0.74
10% Debentures	2,000,000	41.7	5	2.09
	4,800,000	100.0		9.09

We now have a weighted average cost of capital of 9.09 per cent for the highly geared company compared with 11.57 per cent for the company with lower gearing—a quite significant difference—and from this it can be seen that the way in which an organization obtains its funds is important.

The criteria employed in deciding whether to employ equity or borrowed funds may be said to be:

1. The effect of each option on profitability. The earnings per £1 share of equity, i.e., the after-tax profit divided by the number of ordinary shares.
2. The risk inherent in the borrowing option. Whether or not sufficient profits will be made to meet the interest charges and leave some over.
3. The effect of issuing further equity on the existing control of the organization. The holders of the greatest number of ordinary voting shares, i.e., in excess of 50 per cent, have control.
4. The effect of issuing further equity on the asset value per share. Issuing more shares generally reduces the asset value per share as the assets do not normally increase proportionally at once.

The decision will be made as a balancing of these factors together with what the markets will allow the business to do.

SIXTEEN

MANAGEMENT OF WORKING CAPITAL

The working capital of an organization is invested in its stock, debtors and cash. Working capital is calculated as current assets minus current liabilities and its management is highly significant to the survival of any organization. Of the organizations that fail in the UK, 75–80 per cent are profitable at the time that they do so. The problem stems from the fact that the relationship between cash flow and profitability is not fully understood. It may best be illustrated through the following example.

Mr Brown of B Ltd started his financial year in an optimistic frame of mind. He manufactured cheap kitchen aids for which there was a buoyant demand. He sold them for £4 and manufactured them for £3 each. Stock was kept at 30 days, he paid his bills promptly and billed his customers on the basis of 30 days net. Sales were as expected with steady increases predicted and things began well.

1 April	Cash £28,000	Stock £12,000	Debtors £4,000

In April he made and sold 4,000 aids, dispatched them at a cost of £12,000 and collected the money due to him (receivables). He made £4,000 profit and his books showed:

1 May	Cash £20,000	Stock £12,000	Debtors £16,000

In May sales jumped as expected to 6,000 units. Production was increased to maintain the 30-day stock. He made 8,000 units at a cost of £24,000. The money due for the April sales was received. Total profit for the two months £10,000 (£6,000 + £4,000) and his books now showed:

1 June	Cash £12,000	Stock £18,000	Debtors £18,000

June sales increased even more to 8,000 units. He collected the money due to him on time and to maintain the 30-day stock policy 10,000 units were produced. Profit for the month was £8,000 making the total to date £18,000. The books showed:

1 July	Cash £6,000	Stock £24,000	Debtors £32,000

July sales continued the increased to 10,000 units. He collected the money due to him on time and to maintain the 30 day stock policy 12,000 units were produced. Profit for the month was £10,000 making the total to date £28,000. The books showed:

1 August   Cash £2,000   Stock £36,000   Debtors £40,000

August sales increased to 12,000 units. He collected the money due to him on time and produced 14,000 units to maintain the 30 day stock policy. Profit for the month was £12,000 making the total to date £40,000. The books showed:

1 September   Cash £0   Stock £36,000   Debtors £48,000

Balance of stock expressed in £

	April £	May £	June £	July £	August £
Opening	12,000	12,000	18,000	24,000	30,000
Made	12,000	24,000	30,000	36,000	42,000
	24,000	36,000	48,000	60,000	72,000
Sold	12,000	18,000	24,000	30,000	36,000
Closing	12,000	18,000	24,000	30,000	36,000

Cash statement

	April £	May £	June £	July £	August £
Opening balance	28,000	20,000	12,000	6,000	2,000
Add receipts from sales	4,000	16,000	24,000	32,000	40,000
	32,000	36,000	36,000	38,000	42,000
Deduct manufacturing/ distribution costs	12,000	24,000	30,000	36,000	42,000
Balance carried forward	20,000	12,000	6,000	2,000	0

As can be seen, the cash balance is reduced from £28,000 to £0 between April and the end of August. Drastic action is required to control the working capital and prevent the business going into liquidation.

The less money organizations have tied up in stock and the debtors the better, but the economic climate makes it difficult to keep these items down as far as most businesses would wish. Stock levels during the 1980s fell as the result of destocking brought about by the recession so there is less working capital tied up here than was previously the case. Unfortunately the same is not true of debtors. In the 1990s, businesses, desperate to obtain sales, have been forced to extend credit facilities to customers as a way of doing so in a highly competitive environment. This as we have seen gives rise to cash flow problems. One way of dealing with this is to use the services of a factor as mentioned previously on page 4. This would enable you to obtain a large percentage of the money due quickly enough for you to make use of it in running your business. It would have to be paid for but the service is worth its weight in gold for many organizations.

SEVENTEEN
CHANGING PRICE LEVELS

During the late 1980s and early 1990s a great deal has been written about the impact of changing price levels on company profits and liquidity. The accounting bodies as well as individuals have suggested methods of dealing with the problem but no method has been officially recognized by the government. Many organizations carry current cost accounts in their annual report alongside the traditional historical cost reports. However, it is still on the profits as reported in the historical cost accounts that organizations are taxed. In this chapter the Hyde approach to dealing with changing price levels will be discussed and the impact of inflation on profits and liquidity illustrated.

16.1 INFLATION

Inflation has its greatest impact in three main areas, they are:

1. Stock value.
2. Borrowing referred to as gearing. The higher the borrowing the greater the gearing.
3. Replacement costs of assets in the balance sheet and through them the charge for depreciation.

Stock value

Changes in stock value are recorded in the cost of sales adjustment calculated by the average method.

(a) Cost of sales calculated on the historical cost basis:

		(£'000s)
Opening stock		350
Add Stock purchased		2,300
		2,650
Deduct Closing stock		540
Cost of sales historical basis		2,110

Index numbers for cost of stock:
    Start of period   100
    End of period   120
    Average   110

These numbers would be obtained from an index relevant to the organization such as the Retail Price Index.

(b) Revise the opening and closing stock to the average current cost for the year, that is 110:

$$\text{Opening stock } 350 \times \frac{110}{100} = 385$$

$$\text{Closing stock } 540 \times \frac{110}{120} = 495$$

This has the effect of increasing the value of the opening stock and reducing the value of the closing stock to allow for the inflationary impact.

(c) Calculate the current cost of sales using the figures that have just been calculated:

		(£'000s)
Opening stock		385
Add Stock purchased		2,300
		2,685
Deduct Closing stock		495
Cost of sales current cost		2,190

You will see that when the inflationary element is adjusted, the cost of sales increases by £80,000. That is to say the gross profit was previously overstated by that sum and the cost of sales adjustment is:

	(£'000s)
Cost of sales current cost basis	2,190
Cost of sales historical cost basis	2,110
Cost of sales adjustment	80

If the sales had been £4,000 gross profit would be:

Historical cost basis	(£'000s)
Sales	4,000
Cost of sales	2,110
Gross profit	1,890

Current cost basis:	
Sales	4,000
Cost of sales	2,190
Gross profit	1,810

It could be argued that by ignoring the cost of sales adjustment the Inland Revenue is taxing the organization on £80,000 too much profit. The profit is being overstated in real terms by £80,000.

Gearing

Where the total liabilities exceed the total monetary assets after the fixed assets and stock have been adjusted for the difference between current values and historical costs, using a company balance sheet in which the total liabilities are:

	(£'000s)
Equity share capital plus reserves	684
Long-term liabilities	350
Current liabilities	406
	1,440

Fixed assets	600
Stock	540
Monetary assets (e.g., debtors and cash)	300
	1,440

The table is a balance sheet in vertical form of a hypothetical organization; it could just as easily be shown as:

Assets	(£'000s)	Liabilities	(£'000s)
Fixed assets	600	Equity share capital and reserves	684
Stocks	540	Long-term liabilities	350
Monetary assets	300	Current liabilities	406
	1,440		1,440

(a) The net balance of monetary liabilities is calculated as:

	(£'000s)
Long-term liabilities	350
Current liabilities	406
	756
Deduct Monetary assets	300
Net balance of monetary liabilities to outside interests	456

(b) The net balance of monetary liabilities plus equity share capital plus reserves is in this case:

	(£'000s)
Net balance of monetary liabilities	456
Add Equity share capital and reserves	684
	1,140

(c) The gearing proportion, designed to reduce the benefit organizations derive from net borrowings in time of inflation, is then shown to be:

	(£'000s)
Net balance of monetary liabilities	456
Divided by the net balance of monetary liabilities plus equity share capital and reserves	1,140

Expressed in percentage terms to calculate the gearing proportion we have

$$\frac{456 \times 100}{1,140} = 40 \text{ per cent}$$

The cost of sales adjustment and the depreciation adjustment, which we have yet to calculate, work in favour of the organization as they reduce the reported profit on which tax has to be paid. This is because inflation works to overstate the profits made when accounts are prepared on the basis of historical costs. The gearing adjustment works the other way since the benefits derived by organizations that borrow in times of inflation are not shown in accounts that have been prepared on an historical cost basis. This is compensated for by the gearing adjustment which tends to increase profits reported on the historical cost basis.

Depreciation

The depreciation adjustment is calculated in the following way:

(a) From the hypothetical balance sheet we have fixed assets of £600,000 shown at cost.

(b) The replacement cost of the assets is obtained by pricing them (or their nearest equivalent) at today's costs. It may be that they would cost £1,300,000 to replace. That is to say that they are undervalued in the balance sheet on the replacement cost basis by £700,000.

(c) The depreciation adjustment is calculated as illustrated

	(£'000s)
Fixed assets on historical cost basis	600
Fixed assets on replacement cost basis	1,300
	700

Depreciation on additional value at 10 per cent (or whatever the appropriate rate of depreciation is for the assets in question) $\dfrac{10}{100} \times 700,000 = £70,000$.

This shows that the profits have been overstated by £70,000, because of the inflationary impact on the fixed assets, and by £80,000, because of the impact on stocks. Reported profits for tax purposes would be reduced by both these sums. The gearing adjustment works the other way and is, therefore, used to reduce the benefit gained from the stock and depreciation adjustment.

Gearing adjustment	(£'000s)
Depreciation adjustment	70
Cost of sales adjustment	80
	150
Multiply by the gearing proportion	40%
Gearing adjustment	60

The overall impact on the profit of an organization can be illustrated as:

	(£'000s)	(£'000s)
Profit before tax		355
Less adjustments:		
Depreciation	70	
Cost of sales	80	150
	—	—
		205
Add Gearing adjustment		60
		—
Adjusted profit before tax		265
		=

This shows that many organizations are being taxed on inflated rather than on true economic profits but no agreement has yet been reached on what should be done about it.

The impact of inflation on the liquidity of an organization should never be ignored. It is highlighted in the following example which gives a good impression of its effect:

Example *1981–91 10 years of rising prices*

Balance sheet: 1 January

	Cost £'000s	Depn £'000s	1981 £'000s	1991 £'000s		1981 £'000s	1991 £'000s
Factory	100	—	100		Capital	300	
Plant	300	150	150		Reserves	100	
Vehicles	200	100	100		Debentures	100	
	—	—	—				
	600	250	350				
	—	—					
Stock		200			Creditors	113	
Debtors		100			Taxation provision	21	
Cash		5	305		Dividend provision	21	
		—	—	—	Bank overdraft	—	
			655			—	—
			—	=		655	
						—	=

Information 1981–91   General

Indices of Capital Replacement Costs

	January 1981	January 1991	Increase %
Industrial buildings	336	508	51
Industrial plant	377	549	46
Commercial vehicles	293	404	38

Retail Price Index—increase 50 per cent (approx)

Information 1981–91   Specific to above company
Depreciation of plant—straight line basis with estimated life of 10 years.
Depreciation of vehicles—straight line basis with estimated life of 5 years, i.e., plant replaced once, vehicles replaced twice during the decade.

Profit 1981	(10 per cent on capital employed)	50
	Corporation tax 42½ per cent	21.25
		28.75
	Dividend 7 per cent	21.00 (cover 1.4)
	Retained profits	7.75

Assumptions
1. Corporation tax levied at 42½ per cent throughout the decade.
2. Stock costs rose at similar rate to Index of Retail Prices.
3. Company raised its prices at a similar rate, i.e., maintained the real value of its profits.
4. Dividends raised at same rate.

Required
Trace the effects of rising prices on the company in the above model in which the physical level of activity remains constant throughout the ten-year period. The only change occurring is the change in prices.

How has the liquid position of the company changed? Approximate where necessary.

SOLUTION *1981–91 10 years of rising prices*

Balance sheet: 1 January

	Cost £'000s	Depn £'000s	1981 £'000s	1991 £'000s		1981 £'000s	1991 £'000s
Factory	100	—	100	100	Capital	300	300
Plant	300	150	150	219	Reserves	100	196
Vehicles	200	100	100	138	Debentures	100	100
	600	250	350	457			
					Creditors	113	169.5
Stock		200		300	Taxation provision	21	31.5
Debtors		100		150	Dividend provision	21	31.5
Cash		5	305	7.5	Bank overdraft	—	86
			655	914.5		655	914.5

SOLUTION (shown above) is derived as follows:
Factory As this has not been replaced in the period, there is no change and so remains at £100,000.

Plant This was five years old in 1981 and so will have been replaced. The effect is to increase its cost by 46 per cent to £219,000.

Vehicles These were half-way through their life in 1981 and will have been replaced. The effect is to increase their cost by 38 per cent to £138,000.

Stock Constantly replaced. The effect is to increase its value to £300,000, i.e., 50 per cent.

Debtors Constantly replaced. The effect is to increase their value to £150,000, i.e., 50 per cent.

Cash Always circulating. Its value is increased to £7,500 from £5,000; £305,000 is the total of current assets in 1981.

Capital This will not have been replaced in the period and remains at £300,000.

Reserves These will be constantly increasing by the retained profits. The retentions may be roughly calculated as follows:

	1981 £'000s		1991 £'000s
Profit (10 per cent on capital employed)	50	50% inc.	75
Less Corporation tax 42½ per cent	21.25	50% inc.	31.875
	28.75		43.125
Dividend 7 per cent	21	50% inc.	31.5
Retained profits	7.75		11.625

The difference in the retained profits is £3,875; 50 per cent of the difference is £1,937.50. If £1,937.50 is deducted from the new retained profits of £11,625 it gives a rough average increase of £9,600 per annum, which over ten years becomes £96,000 and makes the reserves £100,000 + £96,000 = £196,000.

Debentures. These have not been replaced and so remain constant at £100,000.

Creditors Constantly renewed. The effect is to increase their value to £169,500, i.e. by 50 per cent.

Taxation provision Constantly updated and so increased by the change in the Retail Price Index of 50 per cent to £31,500.

Dividend provision Constantly updated and so increased by 50 per cent to £31,500.

Bank overdraft This is put in as a balancing figure. It can be seen that the cash balance has changed from £5,000 in hand to a bank overdraft figure of £86,000. The liquidity of an apparently successful company has been reduced by £91,000 by the effect of inflation.

This helps to explain why so many organizations are suffering with liquidity problems.

16.2 PROBLEMS CREATED FOR FINANCIAL MANAGERS

Having examined the adjustments caused by inflation we can investigate some of the problems created for financial managers. We will do this by discussing the three main areas.

Stock value

Changes in the value of stock make it difficult to arrive at the charge that should be made against income for the stock that has been used in achieving that income. When too small a charge is made, profits are overstated and too much may be withdrawn from the business by way of dividends, making it hard for the company to maintain its trading position when stocks have to be replaced.

Take an organization that has sales of £100,000 and profits of £10,000. It could be tempted, if it has enough cash, to distribute £8,000 of the £10,000 profit. This may be reasonable in some circumstances, but what if the cost of goods sold calculation (that is opening stock + purchases − closing stock) resulted in a charge of £10,000 while the cost of replacing those goods sold was £15,000. Profit should be reduced by half to £5,000 and the owners persuaded to take far less out of the business or it will not be possible for the organization to purchase enough stock to meet demands for the goods. The financial manager has to tread a careful line between being overcautious and allowing the business to fail through an inability to compete in the market place. Good communication skills are essential to the accountant/manager who has to make others understand the problem and cooperate in overcoming it.

Gearing

The problem for the financial manager with borrowing is not only in arriving at the optimum level to minimize costs but also in the maintenance of sufficient cash flow. Should decisions be taken to maximize borrowing when times are good, then a combination of inflation and poor trading conditions can cause insurmountable problems. In a stable environment an organization could be making profits regularly in the region of £200,000 and generating cash flow of £250,000. This could enable borrowings of £500,000 and interest payments of £50,000 to be easily supported. Changed conditions might cause profits to fall to £150,000 but inflation and the need to extend credit in order to maintain sales in a highly competitive market would have far greater impact on cash generated and could reduce it to £70,000. This would make it difficult for the business to survive, as insufficient money would be available to meet its expenses including interest on borrowing. The financial manager has some very difficult problems to overcome in trying to allow the business to expand while at the same time endeavouring to ensure that it is not vulnerable when conditions change.

Fixed assets

Changes in the value of fixed assets cause problems in arriving at the charge that should be included in each financial period for their use. This charge is made through depreciation and in times of inflation it is all too easy to under-depreciate which gives rise to problems of cash flow. The financial manager is in a quandary as he has to conform with the principle of consistency while at the same time ensuring that a sufficiently large charge is made for depreciation. One way of doing this is to create reserves which reduce profit and by so doing lower the amount available for distribution to the owners of the business.

To make this possible the rest of the management team has to be convinced that the transfer to reserves is a sensible thing to do and not just more trickery on the accountant's behalf. The impact of failing to do so on the business and on the individuals concerned must be clearly explained. This should help to secure cooperation and one way of doing so may be to explain the problem this way:

Asset cost end 1986   £12,000, life ten years, estimated scrap value £2,000
Book value end 1991   £7,000, replacement cost end 1991   £15,000
Total depreciation to date   £5,000
Book value end 1996   £2,000, estimated replacement cost end 1996 £18,000
Total depreciation £10,000

In 1996 the organization will need to find £16,000 to replace the asset. That is the replacement cost of £18,000 less the scrap value of £2,000 but it will only have retained profits of £10,000 through depreciation provision. The depreciation will have helped to strengthen the business but it is doubtful if it will have done so sufficiently for it to generate the cash flow of £16,000 required. The financial manager has somehow to make up that shortfall, either by borrowing or else by internally generated funds. The best way of doing so is by using the business's own resources, but for this to be possible sufficient profits must be retained and not distributed by way of dividends or otherwise. This may be done by transferring an additional £1,200 to reserves in each of the years 1992 to 1996. The cooperation of all concerned must be obtained before anything of this nature can be achieved.

EIGHTEEN

MANAGEMENT INFORMATION TECHNOLOGY
Martyn Roberts, Senior Lecturer
Portsmouth Polytechnic

Information technology has developed to such an extent over the last 10 years that it has become essential for managers to appreciate the ways in which it can assist them in carrying out their tasks. It can be particularly helpful in the preparation of balance sheets, profit statements and cash statements, as well as in financial planning.

There has been a great deal of debate as to the meaning of Information Technology (IT) and many definitions exist, but the one that seems the most appropriate is that by the DTI: '. . . the acquisition, processing, storage and dissemination of information by means of computers and telecommunications'.

Information usually means data, which comprises unadjusted facts and figures, presented in a way that is useful for a particular purpose. It is not a universal concept as information that is useful to one person may be simply seen as data by another. One of the dangers of IT is that information may be produced that is of no use to anybody, thus making the manager suspicious of the whole concept. Managers must guard against being overwhelmed with unnecessary information.

The various components of IT and their application to the working manager will be explored in this chapter, and some commonly met terms explained.

18.1 COMPUTER HARDWARE

This is the term to describe the physical components that make up the computer. It is conventionally broken down into four identifiable areas: input, output, central processing unit and secondary storage.

Input

These are devices that allow data to be input to the computer. Frequently a keyboard is used, but devices such as a 'mouse' or lightpen are also used.

Output

There are devices that present the processed data to the user.

Visual display unit (VDU)   The VDU consists of a monitor and a keyboard. Until recently most monitors were monochrome (one colour against a dark background), but now colour monitors are becoming more common. One full screen is normally 24 rows by 80 columns. The image presented on the screen consists of a number of dots known as pixels. The greater the number of pixels the greater the resolution of the screen. A monitor can be given a higher resolution by fitting a special circuit board inside the personal computer (PC): An EGA (enhanced graphics adaptor) has 640×225 pixels; VGA (video graphics adaptor) has 640×430 pixels. This allows the use of powerful graphical software.

Printers   A printer is essential for any business computer. There are a number of types available and the manager's choice will be dependent on the types of applications likely to be run and the budget allowance.

1.   *Dot matrix*   The dot matrix is the workhorse of most systems. Recent advances in technology have meant that modern dot matrix printers are extremely versatile, capable of printing characters in a variety of fonts and pitches to an extremely high quality. They are also capable of printing graphics. They are fast (up to 400 characters per second (cps)) and relatively inexpensive (up to £500).

2.   *Daisy wheel*   This is so called because of the shape of the print head which is essentially a disk with thin arms (petals) containing characters. The disk spins to the required character and a hammer strikes the print head against the ribbon and paper. It is used essentially for high quality letter output but tends to be slow (50 cps), noisy and limited to non-graphical applications. The daisy wheel is now rapidly becoming obsolete due to advances in other types of printers.

3.   *Laser*   Falling prices together with advances in technology have combined to ensure that these printers are becoming as popular as dot matrix. The technology is very similar to that of the photocopier, resulting in high quality output produced very quickly with little noise. They are useful for both text and graphics output.

4.   *Inkjet*   The inkjet is an alternative to the laser. It operates by squirting tiny droplets of electrostatically charged ink onto paper. These printers produce high quality output quickly and noiselessly and many have the capability to print in colour.

Central processing unit (CPU)

The CPU is the part of the computer that actually processes data. It consists of two parts: the processor and memory.

Microprocessor   In the modern PC the CPU is a very small electronic component known as the microprocessor. The microprocessor combines the arithmetic/logic unit which actually performs calculations and comparisons on data and the control unit which coordinates operations throughout the entire computer system.

Main memory (random access memory RAM)   This is where programs and data are stored for immediate use. It consists of a number of specialized memory chips (components) which can be accessed very quickly. Most microcomputers have a minimum of 512K of RAM (random-access memory) but the latest machines can accommodate up to 16Mb. Generally speaking the more RAM a computer has the faster applications are likely to work. RAM is said to be volatile which means that when the power supply is switched off the contents of RAM will be lost.

Read only memory (ROM)   ROM is not available to the user but is used to store essential operating system instructions.

Secondary storage

Main memory is limited in size and is volatile. Therefore another more permanent method of storing programs and data is required. This is done through the use of secondary storage. Modern microcomputers usually incorporate a hard (Winchester) disk which is held within the system unit. The disk normally has a capacity of between 20 and 100 Mb and provides reasonably fast access times. The alternative storage device is a floppy disk which tends to be used these days to back-up the hard disk. These have much less storage capacity — up to 1.44 Mb—and the access time is considerably slower. They do have the advantage that they can be stored at some distance from the computer for security purposes.

18.2 COMPUTER SOFTWARE

Software is the term used to describe the programs and instructions which tell the hardware what to do. Without software of some description the computer is of no use. Software is basically of two types: system software and application software.

System software

Before a computer is useable an operating system must be loaded. This is software which controls the operation of a computer to make the most efficient use of the resources available. The most popular operating system for microcomputers is DOS (disk operating system) but other operating systems such as OS/2 and UNIX are gaining popularity.

Application software

These are the programs and instructions designed to carry out tasks for particular applications (e.g., invoicing). Good application software makes the computer an extremely friendly tool to use.

Software tools   Application software can be of two types: either bespoked, i.e., written from scratch for a particular user/application, or packaged, i.e., purchased off the shelf in a form ready to use immediately. Bespoked software can be produced using a number of software development tools: spreadsheets, database management systems, integrated packages.

1.   *Spreadsheets*   Spreadsheets are not a new idea: pen and paper spreadsheets have been used by businesses for centuries. A spreadsheet is basically a worksheet divided into a series of rows and columns used for organizing and displaying numeric and textual information. What is new is the electronic spreadsheet. Using the spreadsheet the user builds a model to meet a particular application requirement.

The electronic spreadsheet has numerous advantages over the old manual version. Formulae can be built into the model so that any calculations will be performed automatically irrespective of the data being used. Any corrections to errors or amendments to the model can be made easily, without having to start afresh. The spreadsheet model and data can be stored on disk to be used over and over again. Perhaps the greatest advantage of all is that if one data value or formula in the model is changed all other values in the model are recalculated automatically to reflect the change. This factor can be put to good use in assisting managers to perform 'what-if' analysis. This is the process where one formula or value is changed in the model and the effect on all other values is immediately visible, thus assisting the user to select the best alternative from a number of options.

Spreadsheet software is extremely versatile, capable of being used by many financial applications. The technology has now advanced to the point where most spreadsheets include advanced facilities such as statistical functions (regression, etc.) database functions and powerful graphics facilities. Here in Fig. 18.1(a) and (b) are a sample of the many applications of spreadsheets.

	Qtr. 1	Qtr. 2	Qtr. 3	Qtr. 4
Revenue Prod 1	100	120	140	160
Prod 2	100	120	140	160
Prod 3	100	120	140	160
Total Revenue	300	360	420	480
Costs:				
salaries	50	50	60	80
rent	50	60	70	80
motor	10	20	30	40
misc.	10	10	15	15
Total costs	120	140	175	215
Profit	180	220	245	265

(a)

Figure 18.1   Two suggested applications of spreadsheets (a) and (b)

	8	0	2	5
1	QTR. 1	QTR. 2	QTR. 3	QTR. 4
2	==================================			
3 REVENUE				
4 PROD 1	100	120	140	160
5 PROD 2	100	120	140	160
6 PROD 3	100	120	140	160
7	==================================			
8 TOTAL REVENUE	300	360	420	480
9				
10 COSTS:				
11 SALARIES	50	50	60	80
12 RENT	50	60	70	80
13 MOTOR	10	20	30	40
14 MISC.	10	10	15	15
15	==================================			
16	120	140	175	215
17				
18 PROFIT	180	220	245	265

(b)

Figure 18.1

Financial statements   The statutory financial statements of most organizations (balance sheet, profit and loss account, etc.) can easily be assembled on a spreadsheet. The spreadsheet has the advantage of being able to calculate subtotals and grand totals so that if a change to any one figure within the statement is made the totals will automatically be updated. Also by using the 'move' facility we can change the layout of the statement easily. It has often been said, 'profit is a subjective figure'. By using a spreadsheet we can perform 'what-if' calculations to produce the desired profit figure. This is of relevance to the examples given in Chapter 2 The Balance Sheet, Chapter 3 The Income Statement and Chapter 6 Funds Flow.

Cash budgets   The spreadsheet provides an ideal tool to calculate receipts and payments over a future period of time. Using the spreadsheet we can calculate the cash requirements of the organization. This is particularly applicable to the examples in Chapter 4.

Capital budgeting   Most spreadsheets now incorporate functions to calculate net present values and internal rates of return which can reduce a great deal of the work undertaken in the examples in Chapter 13.

Ratio analysis   Using a spreadsheet we can analyse and compare the financial statements of organizations which would be helpful in assessing the information in Chapters 5 and 19. It is important to remember however that it is the manager who makes the final decisions by applying his or her specialist skills. No program has yet been written that is capable of replacing the manager in the decision-making process.

Database Management Systems (DBMS)   DBMS are pieces of software that allow data to be organized and stored in a manner which allows fast and easy retrieval. In essence the DBMS is a very efficient filing system. A DBMS is a major benefit where an organization has large volumes of data to be stored. The DBMS will include facilities to allow data to be retrieved from the database that matches specified criteria given by the user.

```
Structure of a database file using dBase IV / Ashton/Tate

Page £      1

Structure for database: C:/D1.DBF
Number of data records:
Date of last update    : 02/05/91
Field   Field         Type          Width      Dec      Index
        Name
   1    SNAME         Character       20                   N
   2    FNAME         Character       20                   N
   3    TITLE         Character        4                   N
   4    ADD1          Character       20                   N
   5    ADD2          Character       20                   N
   6    ADD3          Character       20                   N
   7    ADD4          Character       20                   N
   8    TELNO         Character       18                   N
   9    AGE           Numeric          2                   N
  10    DOB           Date             8                   N
** Total **                          153
```

Figure 18.2   Structure of a database file

Popular DBMS for microcomputers include dBASEII, III and IV, Paradox, Delta and Foxpro. The advantages of using a DBMS other than the speed of data retrieval element include:

Reduced redundancy   Where organizations have many files containing data it is not unusual for a piece of data to be stored more than once in many different files. Using a DBMS a piece of data will only be stored once. This will make updating records much easier and will reduce the amount of erroneous data within the database.

Shared data   Conceptually the database is simply a common pool of data. If the database is installed on a multi-user computer or if PCs are linked together (networked) then the database is accessible by many persons within an organization.

Integrated files   Many DBMS support relational databases. By relational we mean that the database consists of a number of separate files of data and each file is related to one or more other files in some way. The DBMS will join the related files together when required. For example, imagine a manufacturing organization which takes orders and each order is from a particular customer. Normally there would be one file for orders and one file for customers. Suppose you wanted to know the address of the customer who had placed a particular order. In a manual system you would have to look first in the folder or drawer containing orders to find the order you are interested in and then having found the order note down the name of the customer and look in the customer folder/drawer to find the relevant address. Using a relational DBMS, because the files are linked, you would get the customer address instantly you called up an order.

Security and control   The DBMS will maintain the integrity of the database. It will ensure data is stored in the right format at the correct intervals. A good DBMS will also include facilities to ensure only those persons authorized to have access to the database are actually allowed entry. This is particularly important for sensitive items such as marketing, sales, personnel and payroll data.

With a DBMS it is possible for end users to maintain simple files of data (e.g. a customer file) or to build quite complex and sophisticated systems (e.g. an accounting system). The level at which it is used depends upon the skill and expertise of the end user but there comes a point for most users when it becomes economical to purchase a prewritten application package.

Integrated packages   These are pieces of software which normally incorporate a spreadsheet, DBMS and word processor within one package. To some extent Lotus 1-2-3 is an integrated package in that it incorporates a spreadsheet, a simple DBMS and graphics facilities, but in Lotus some of these features are quite limited. Other integrated packages such as Symphony, Open Access and Framework take the idea much further and include a word processor as well as good graphics, DBMS and spreadsheet.

Integrated packages make the task of transferring data/text between modules extremely simple. They also offer the advantage of ease of use having commonly used pieces of software within one package but it is likely that any one facility will be less powerful than the equivalent dedicated package.

Application packages

These are pieces of software written specifically for particular applications. For the purpose of this book, only Accounts packages are discussed. However, the list of specialist application packages is virtually endless and it includes such areas as personnel, production control, stock control, hotel room booking and medical practice systems, to name but a few. The power and sophistication of such packages is improving all the time. As with other packages they can be purchased 'off the shelf' ready for immediate use.

Accounts systems   Now widely used by businesses, most modern accounts systems are designed in a modular fashion; that is, an organization can purchase one or more discrete modules and build a system to meet their own particular needs. Modules commonly have the facility to be linked together thus forming an integrated system. Examples of modules include nominal ledger, sales ledger, purchase ledger, invoicing, order processing, payroll and job costing.

The major advantage of using a computerized accounts package as opposed to a traditional manual system is the ease of generation of information for management. From the raw data entered into the system it is simply a matter of pressing a button to produce sales listings, debtors reports, analyses and so on. Also details of particular transactions can be retrieved and examined much faster than with traditional ledger books and folders of invoices. Popular accounts systems include Sage, Pegasus, Multisoft and Tetra.

Expert systems   An expert system is a software package used with an extensive set of organized data that presents the computer as an expert on some topic. The user is the knowledge seeker, usually asking questions in a natural, English-like, language format. An expert can respond to an inquiry with both an answer and an explanation of the answer. The expert system works by figuring out what the question means and then matching it against the facts and rules it knows.

Expert systems are now being used extensively in the financial area to complement the work of accountants, tax planners and company lawyers.

18.3 COMMUNICATIONS

Referring back to the original definition of IT, the words '. . . dissemination of information by computers and telecommunications' were used. Communications between computers over a distance are now an essential element of many organizations. Telecommunications offer enormous gains in terms of improvements in the speed of transfer of data, enabling management to have up-to-date information at their finger tips.

Local area networks (LANS)

This is the process of linking together PCs in one particular geographical location. Once PCs are linked users can have immediate access to common files, users can share peripheral devices (e.g., high quality printers), and can pass data to each other with ease. Common network systems include Ethernet, IBM Token Ring and Cambridge Ring.

Wide area networks (WANS)

This is where computer equipment is linked together over a large distance using communication equipment provided by some third party organization (e.g., British Telecom, Mercury). The simplest way to link computers is to use the standard telephone network and a piece of equipment called a MODEM which converts signals used by a computer to those suitable for transfer along a telephone line. This is relatively inexpensive if the volume of data to be transferred is small but the speed of transfer is slow and it becomes uneconomic for high usage. Another way is to use the packet switched stream facility (PSS). This is a service dedicated for the transmission of computer signals. Essentially the data from the computer is assembled into packets which, as well as containing data, are labelled with the address of the recipient. The packets are put onto the network and travel along until they arrive at their destination. To use this service users pay a rental fee for connection to the network plus a charge for each packet sent. For high volumes of data or for data which has to be transferred extremely quickly dedicated telecommunication lines can be leased.

REFERENCES

Anderson, R., *Business Systems and Information Technology*, Paradigm, London, 1988.
Blewett, F., and R. Jarvis, *Microcomputing in Accounting*, Van Nostrand Reinhold (International), London, 1989.
Capron, H. L., *Computers: Tools for an Information Age*, Benjamin Cummings, California, 1990.
Curtis, G., *Business Information Systems*, Addison-Wesley, Wokingham, 1989.

NINETEEN

PERFORMANCE ANALYSIS

In Chapter 5 we looked at some of the ways in which financial information can be used and interpreted by managers. This will be put on a more formalized basis in this chapter with the introduction of a 'ratio tree' for the manufacturing industry (Figure 19.1).

The ratio tree can be used as a useful diagnostic tool. If your primary ratio of operating profit to net capital employed is giving the desired return of, say, 18 per cent then there is no need for any investigation. If, on the other hand, the return is 5 per cent when 18 per cent was expected, something has gone seriously wrong and further investigation is necessary. The supporting ratios will be explored next to see if either or both are giving unexpected results. When the ratio of operating profit to sales is satisfactory it is not necessary to investigate any of the ratios that lead up to it, that is (3-1), (3-2), (3-3), (4-1), (4-2), (4-3), (4-4); should the ratio of sales to net assets employed figure be unsatisfactory then ratio (3-4) will be calculated. If it is unsatisfactory, attention will have to be concentrated on sales as little can be done with fixed capital in the short term. It may be that sales have fallen dramatically so that a drive is necessary to build them up or, if the product mix is wrong, it may be necessary to market an entirely new product. Should the sales to fixed capital ratio be unsatisfactory, then the sales to working capital ratio will be calculated, followed by the ratios (4-5), (4-6), (4-7), (4-8) and (4-9), whichever of the ratios are showing warning signals. Once the cause of the problem has been discovered the action necessary to correct it can be instigated or, if that is not possible, the business may have to be sold.

If, on the other hand, the problem is shown to be on the operating profit to sales side of the tree then the investigation will follow the ratios (3-1), (3-2), (3-3) and if these do not explain the cause of the problem the operating level ratios (4-1), (4-2), (4-3) and (4-4) will be calculated. This should reveal the cause of the problem and enable corrective action to be taken. The example at the foot of the tree illustrates the terms in which the ratios are expressed. It is *not* a guide as to the magnitude of the ratio. No such guide can be issued as each sector has its own rule of thumb measure. Tracing the ratios through we see that they are expressed in the following terms:

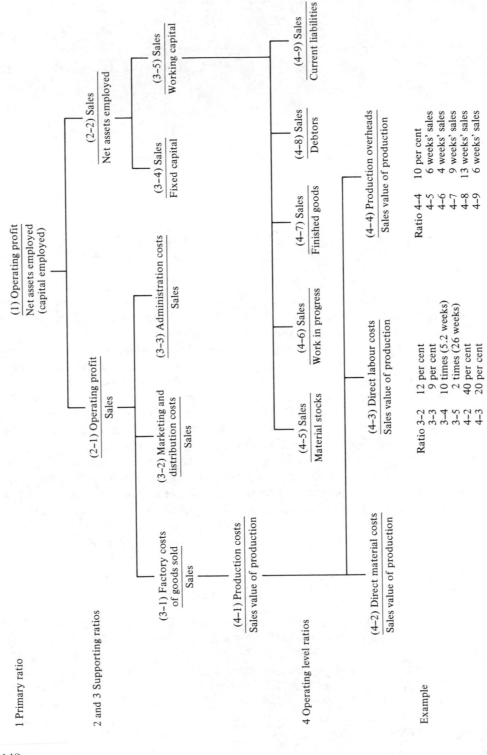

Figure 19.1 Accounting Ratios – Manufacturing Industry (Ratio Tree)

148

(3-2) $$\frac{\text{Marketing and distribution costs} \times 100}{\text{Sales}} = \text{Percentage of sales}$$

(3-3) $$\frac{\text{Admin. costs} \times 100}{\text{Sales}} = \text{Percentage of sales}$$

(3-4) $$\frac{\text{Sales}}{\text{Fixed capital}} = \text{Times turned over} \qquad \frac{52 \text{ weeks}}{\text{Times turned over}} = \text{Weeks to turn over the fixed capital}$$

(3-5) $$\frac{\text{Sales}}{\text{Working capital}} = \text{Times turned over} \qquad \frac{52 \text{ weeks}}{\text{Times turned over}} = \text{Weeks to turn over the working capital}$$

(4-2) $$\frac{\text{Direct material cost} \times 100}{\text{Sales value of production}} = \text{Percentage of the sales value of production made up of the direct material cost}$$

(4-3) $$\frac{\text{Direct labour cost} \times 100}{\text{Sales value of production}} = \text{Percentage of the sales value of production made up of the direct labour cost}$$

(4-4) $$\frac{\text{Production overheads} \times 100}{\text{Sales value of production}} = \text{Percentage of the sales value of production made up of the production overheads}$$

(4-5) $$\frac{\text{Sales}}{\text{Material stocks}} = \text{Times material stocks are turned over} \qquad \frac{52 \text{ weeks}}{\text{Times turned over}} = \text{Weeks' sales held in stock}$$

(4-6) $$\frac{\text{Sales}}{\text{Work in progress}} = \text{Times work in progress turned over} \qquad \frac{52 \text{ weeks}}{\text{Times turned over}} = \text{Weeks' sales held in WIP}$$

(4-7) $$\frac{\text{Sales}}{\text{Finished goods}} = \text{Times finished goods turned over} \qquad \frac{52 \text{ weeks}}{\text{Times turned over}} = \text{Weeks' sales held in finished goods}$$

(4-8) $$\frac{\text{Sales}}{\text{Debtors}} = \text{Times debtors turned over} \qquad \frac{52 \text{ weeks}}{\text{Times turned over}} = \text{Weeks taken to collect money from your customers}$$

(4-9) $$\frac{\text{Sales}}{\text{Current liabilities}} = \text{Times current liabilities turned over} \qquad \frac{52 \text{ weeks}}{\text{Times turned over}} = \text{Weeks taken to cover your current liabilities in sales}$$

PERFORMANCE ANALYSIS QUESTION

Electronic Appliances Ltd

Mr Wright, the Managing Director of Electronic Appliances Ltd, manufacturers of electronic control equipment, is reviewing the progress of his company which he established ten years ago in London. It is a public company and he has plans to obtain a Stock Exchange quotation in about two years' time. In view of this Mr Wright believes he should increase his dividend as much as possible; no interim dividends are paid, only the final dividend.

He is an inventive man, and a first-class engineer. He has an excellent and rapidly growing development and design department, and in the last three years he has produced some very sophisticated equipment. This increase in range has not only been through increasing the size range of each item, but also the number of new items now is four times what it was three years ago. He prides himself that his company could design almost anything of the highest quality that a customer would require in electronic controls. This viewpoint is well founded, for the company has a high reputation for inventive skills and is often consulted by private and government agencies.

His sales force has more than doubled over the last three years, and he now has seven technical representatives covering the UK and abroad. His customers are widely spread, both geographically and in the range of industries served.

His manufacturing plant is becoming very efficient, and two years ago a high degree of automation was introduced into the factory. He has doubled the output of his company but has only increased his total staff by 50 per cent over the last three years. The stock figures in the balance sheet represent materials, components and bought out sub-assemblies; none represents finished work.

Yet despite all this success his bank manager, who has just received the company's latest profit and loss account and balance sheet, has asked Mr Wright to call at the bank at 4.00 p.m. on Wednesday, 12 March, as the bank is seriously concerned with the state of his company, and requires a substantial reduction in the overdraft, which has now risen to £180,000 at close of bank business on Monday, 10 March. In September last year the overdraft limit was raised from £100,000 to £160,000.

The accounts and operating data of Electronic Appliances Ltd for the last three years of operation are shown on pages 151–155. Analyse these figures and relate them to the above information known about the company and its Managing Director.

(a) Assume you are Mr Wright and marshal the facts, figures, plans and ideas in the most favourable light to persuade the bank to keep (or even to raise) the current overdraft limits
(b) Assume you are the bank manager and critically assess the company's performance before deciding what action you believe is appropriate.

Electronic Appliances Ltd

Balance sheet—31 December 1989

CAPITAL EMPLOYED	£	£	£
Issued capital and reserves			
340,000 50p ordinary shares			170,000
General reserves			300,000
Share premium account			30,327
Balance profit and loss account			30,217
			530,544

EMPLOYMENT OF CAPITAL			
Fixed assets:			
Buildings		182,054	
Plant		120,265	
Vehicles		8,162	310,481
Current assets:			
Work in progress	106,203		
Stocks (finished goods)	71,019		
Debtors	105,001		
Bank	1,050	283,273	
Current liabilities:			
Creditors	32,546		
Tax	30,664	63,210	220,063
			530,544

Electronic Appliances Ltd

Balance sheet—31 December 1990

CAPITAL EMPLOYED	£	£	£
Issued capital and reserves			
540,000 50p Ordinary shares			270,000
Share premium account			405,000
General reserves			300,000
Balance profit and loss account			51,018
			1,026,018

EMPLOYMENT OF CAPITAL	£	£	£
Fixed assets:			
Buildings		215,056	
Plant		463,472	
Vehicles		9,890	688,418
Current assets:			
Work in progress	176,321		
Stocks	110,984		
Debtors	154,968		
Bank	1,283	443,556	
Current liabilities:			
Creditors	43,625		
Tax	35,331		
Dividends 10 per cent	27,000	105,956	337,600
			1,026,018

Electronic Appliances Ltd

Balance sheet—31 December 1991

CAPITAL EMPLOYED	£	£	£
Issued capital and reserves			
540,000 50p Ordinary shares			270,000
Share premium account			405,000
General reserves			300,000
Profit and loss account			60,643
			1,035,643

EMPLOYMENT OF CAPITAL			
Fixed assets:			
Buildings		235,125	
Plant		456,684	
Vehicles		11,034	702,843
Current assets:			
Work in progress	246,105		
Stocks	171,864		
Debtors	216,031	634,000	
Current liabilities:			
Creditors	53,201		
Tax	44,852		
Dividends 15 per cent	40,500		
Bank overdraft	162,647	301,200	332,800
			1,035,643

Profit and loss accounts for year ended 31 December

	1989		1990		1991	
	£	£	£	£	£	£
SALES		500,607		699,231		899,698
PRODUCTION COSTS— DIRECT						
Materials	115,321		153,875		186,436	
Labour	70,653		87,487		103,502	
		185,974		241,362		289,938
PRODUCTION COSTS— INDIRECT						
Salaries	27,000		31,800		35,000	
Sages	38,200		68,500		100,200	
Indirect materials	13,500		29,500		45,500	
Tools	6,500		8,500		10,500	
Other expenses	12,280		17,568		22,940	
Depreciation	14,300		34,000		57,000	
Heating	19,000		23,000		24,000	
		130,780		212,868		295,140
TECHNICAL DEPART- MENT (including inspection)						
Salaries	20,820		33,700		51,490	
Wages	4,840		8,860		10,400	
Materials	1,800		4,770		5,200	
Other expenses	7,684		11,201		13,267	
Depreciation	960		1,590		2,100	
		36,104		60,121		82,457

	1989 £	1989 £	1990 £	1990 £	1991 £	1991 £
SALES DEPARTMENT						
Technical representatives	7,185		11,108		17,863	
Representatives' expenses	2,835		4,682		6,947	
Exhibitions	6,243		9,235		15,386	
Advertising	3,820		6,461		7,010	
Sales office salaries	4,187		6,914		8,964	
Other expenses	6,600		10,350		13,100	
Depreciation	212		240		415	
		31,082		48,990		69,685
GENERAL ADMIN-ISTRATION						
Managing director	17,500		20,100		21,800	
Secretary and chauffeur	11,890		15,040		17,740	
Accounts accountant, ledger, cost, wages and cashiers clerks						
Other admin. costs	10,072		17,031		16,637	
Depreciation	545		587		912	
Bank interest	—		—		10,412	
		40,007		52,758		67,501
TOTAL COSTS		423,947		616,099		804,721
PROFIT		£76,660		£83,132		£94,97

155

SUGGESTED ANSWER

Electronic Appliances Ltd

Profitability ratios		1989	1990	1991	
Return on capital employed %		14.5	8.1	9.2	
Profit margin %		15.3	11.9	10.6	
					(Prime costs—under control)
Overheads:					
Production %		26.2	30.4	32.8	
Technical dept %		7.2	8.6	9.2	
Sales dept %		6.2	7.0	7.7	
Capital turnover	Times	0.94	0.68	0.87	
Work in progress	Months	6.9	8.8	10.2	valued at direct cost
Work in progress	Months	4.0	4.6	5.0	valued at prod. cost
Stocks	Months	7.4	8.6	11.1	compared with actual cost
Debtors	Months	2.5	2.7	2.9	
Fixed capital	Months	7.5	12.0	9.4	
Liquidity ratios					
Current ratio	Times	4.5	4.2	2.1	
Acid test ratio	Times	1.7	1.5	0.72	

Application of funds statement 1991

	£	£
Opening liquidity		1,283
Add		
Profit	94,977	
Depreciation	60,427	155,404
		156,687
Deduct		
Tax paid	35,331	
Dividends paid	27,000	
Fixed assets purchased	74,852	137,183
		19,504
Change in working capital		
Increase in WIP	69,784	
Increase in stocks	60,880	
Increase in debtors	61,063	
– Increase in creditors	–9,576	182,151
Closing liquidity—Overdraft		(162,647)

Analysis

The return on capital employed shows a large decline between 1989 and 1990, 14.5 per cent down to 8 per cent, and then a slight recovery to 9.2 per cent in 1991.

The profit margin reflects a similar decline from 15.3 per cent to 10.6 per cent over the three years, although the decline is much greater between 1989 and 1990.

The prime costs are under control and increase in the proportions expected to support the increased sales.

The overheads for the production, technical and sales departments are all increasing steadily and will need to be controlled in future.

The rates of capital turnover are slowing, most noticeably in the case of work in progress and stocks.

The liquidity ratios are declining and the business is obviously failing to generate sufficient funds for its needs. It gives every impression of being an organization run by an enthusiast to meet his needs. He will take on any work that he sees to be a challenge, which maintains his interest and enthusiasm but this is bad for the business.

He needs to decide what his business is about and endeavour to achieve longer runs. This will reduce his overhead costs per unit produced and increase the overall efficiency of the organization.

The calculations for 1989 have been made on the basis shown below.

Return on capital employed $\dfrac{76,660}{530,544} \times 100$ = 14.5 per cent

Profit margin (sales) $\dfrac{76,660}{500,607} \times 100$ = 15.3 per cent

Overheads (sales):

Production $\dfrac{130,780}{500,607} \times 100$ = 26.2 per cent

Technical $\dfrac{36,104}{500,607} \times 100$ = 7.2 per cent

Sales $\dfrac{31,082}{500,607} \times 100$ = 6.2 per cent

Capital turnover $\dfrac{500,607}{530,544}$ = 0.94 times

Work in progress (at direct cost) $\dfrac{185,974}{106,203}$ = 1.75 times $\dfrac{12}{1.75}$ months = 6.9 months

Work in progress (at production cost) $\dfrac{(185,974 + 130,780)}{106,203}$ = 2.98 times $\dfrac{12}{2.98}$ = 4 months

Stocks (at actual cost = materials) $\dfrac{115,321}{71,019}$ = 1.62 times $\dfrac{12}{1.62}$ = 7.4 months

Debtors $\dfrac{500,607}{105,001}$ = 4.77 times $\dfrac{12}{4.77}$ = 2.5 months

Fixed capital (fixed assets) $\dfrac{500,607}{310,481}$ = 1.61 times $\dfrac{12}{1.61}$ = 7.5 months

The other ratios have all been fully investigated earlier.

The following financial statements (pages 159–178) have been copied from the published accounts of Marks and Spencer plc and are included for you to read and analyse using as many of the ratios as you feel necessary to give a good feel for the organization. Compare the results with those of other organizations in the same field and draw your own conclusions using the information that you consider relevant, including the five-year record which provides trends and source and application of funds statement.

REPORT OF THE AUDITORS
To the Members of Marks and Spencer plc

We have audited the financial statements on pages 38 to 57 in accordance with Auditing Standards.

In our opinion the financial statements give a true and fair view of the state of affairs of the Company and the Group at 31 March 1991 and of the profit and source and application of funds of the Group for the year then ended and have been properly prepared in accordance with the Companies Act 1985.

COOPERS & LYBRAND DELOITTE
Chartered Accountants
London 13 May 1991

CONSOLIDATED PROFIT AND LOSS ACCOUNT
For the year ended 31 March 1991

	Notes	1991 £m	1990 £m
Turnover	2	**5,774·8**	5,608·1
Cost of sales		**3,864·1**	3,768·5
Gross profit		**1,910·7**	1,839·6
Other expenses	3	**1,277·2**	1,211·9
Operating profit	6	**633·5**	627·7
Net interest receivable/(payable)	4	**13·3**	(8·8)
Profit before profit sharing and taxation		**646·8**	618·9
Profit sharing		**15·3**	14·7
Profit before exceptional charge and taxation		**631·5**	604·2
Exceptional charge	5	**16·0**	—
Profit on ordinary activities before taxation	6	**615·5**	604·2
Tax on profit on ordinary activities	7	**215·8**	214·5
Profit on ordinary activities after taxation		**399·7**	389·7
Minority interests		**2·4**	0·7
Profit for the financial year	8	**397·3**	389·0
Dividends			
Preference shares		**0·1**	0·1
Ordinary shares:			
Interim of 2·0p per share		**54·3**	49·8
Final of 4·7p per share		**127·6**	122·6
		182·0	172·5
Undistributed surplus	23	**215·3**	216·5
Earnings per share:			
Pre exceptional charge	9	**15·1p**	14·5p
Post exceptional charge	9	**14·7p**	14·5p

BALANCE SHEETS
At 31 March 1991

	Notes	The Group 1991 £m	The Group 1990 £m (restated)	The Company 1991 £m	The Company 1990 £m
Fixed assets					
Tangible assets:					
Land and buildings		**2,193·0**	2,093·9	**2,043·3**	1,958·6
Fixtures, fittings and equipment		**357·8**	343·3	**307·1**	292·8
Assets in the course of construction		**61·8**	31·3	**51·4**	25·7
	13	**2,612·6**	2,468·5	**2,401·8**	2,277·1
Investments	14	**—**	—	**535·2**	433·4
		2,612·6	2,468·5	**2,937·0**	2,710·5
Current assets					
Stocks	15	**351·1**	374·3	**235·8**	268·7
Debtors	16	**617·7**	537·6	**653·9**	640·3
Investments	17	**28·8**	28·1	**12·4**	19·1
Cash at bank and in hand	18	**293·0**	266·6	**41·4**	33·4
		1,290·6	1,206·6	**953·5**	961·5
Current liabilities					
Creditors: amounts falling due within one year	19	**896·7**	925·0	**714·3**	751·2
Net current assets		**393·9**	281·6	239·2	210·3
Total assets less current liabilities		**3,006·5**	2,750·1	**3,176·2**	2,920·8
Creditors: amounts falling due after more			565·2		
than one year	20	**549·6**	4·3	**290·0**	290·0
Provisions for liabilities and charges	21	**19·1**		**16·0**	—
Net assets		**2,437·8**	2,180·6	**2,870·2**	2,630·8
Capital and reserves					
Called up share capital	22	**680·1**	675·0	**680·1**	675·0
Share premium account	23	**69·3**	50·0	**69·3**	50·0
Revaluation reserve	23	**459·7**	458·0	**470·8**	479·4
Profit and loss account	23	**1,218·3**	991·6	**1,650·0**	1,426·4
Shareholders' funds	23	**2,427·4**	2,174·6	**2,870·2**	2,630·8
Minority interests		**10·4**	6·0	**—**	—
Total capital employed		**2,437·8**	2,180·6	**2·870·2**	2,630·8

Approved by the Board
13 May 1991

R Greenbury, CHAIRMAN
J K Oates, MANAGING DIRECTOR

CONSOLIDATED SOURCE AND APPLICATION OF FUNDS
For the year ended 31 March 1991

	1991 £m	1990 £m
Cash and short-term funds at 1 April	**207·3**	44·0
Source of funds		
Arising from trading:		
Profit on ordinary activities before taxation	**615·5**	604·2
Depreciation	**115·9**	109·4
Loss on disposal of fixed assets	**4·7**	7·4
Exceptional charge (see note 5)	**16·0**	—
	752·1	721·0
From other sources:		
Shares issued under share schemes	**24·4**	18·2
Cash and investments in subsidiaries acquired	**—**	1·6
Sales of fixed assets	**16·3**	6·6
Miscellaneous	**5·2**	(5·6)
	45·9	20·8
	1,005·3	785·8
Application of funds		
Payments of dividends (excluding dividends taken in shares)	**164·5**	141·6
Payment of taxation	**231·9**	188·8
Purchase of fixed assets	**300·4**	277·5
Repayment of debenture loan	**5·0**	—
Acquisition of subsidiaries	**—**	3·0
	701·8	608·9
Increase/(decrease) in working capital		
Stocks	**(23·2)**	3·3
Debtors (excluding taxation)	**70·4**	47·2
Creditors due within one year (excluding taxation and dividends)	**34·5**	(80·9)
	81·7	(30·4)
	783·5	578·5
Cash and short-term funds at 31 March	**221·8**	207·3

Cash and short-term funds comprise cash at bank and in hand and current asset investments less bank loans, overdrafts and commercial paper repayable within one year.

ACCOUNTING POLICIES

The financial statements have been prepared in accordance with Statements of Standard Accounting Practice issued by UK accountancy bodies. The principal accounting policies adopted are described below.

Basis of accounting
The financial statements are drawn up on the historical cost basis of accounting modified to include the valuation of certain United Kingdom properties at 31 March 1988.

Basis of consolidation
The Group financial statements incorporate the financial statements of Marks and Spencer plc and all its subsidiaries for the year ended 31 March 1991. The net assets of financial activities were previously shown as a separate item in the Group's balance sheet and analysed in a note. In accordance with the new requirements of the Companies Act 1985, financial activities are now fully consolidated within the main balance sheet. Comparative figures have been restated to reflect the change in policy from last year.

Goodwill
Goodwill arising on consolidation, which represents the difference between the consideration given and the fair value of the net tangible assets acquired, is taken to reserves on acquisition. The net assets of companies acquired are incorporated into the consolidated accounts at their fair values to the Group and after adjustments to bring the accounting policies of companies acquired into alignment with those of the Group.

Deferred taxation
Deferred taxation is provided at anticipated tax rates on differences arising from the inclusion of items of income and expenditure in taxation computations in periods different from those in which they are included in the financial statements. Provision is made on the extent that it is likely that a liability or asset will crystallise in the future.

Depreciation
Depreciation is provided to write off the cost or valuation of tangible fixed assets by equal annual instalments at the following rates:
Freehold and leasehold land and buildings over 50 years — 1 per cent (see *a* below).

Leasehold land and buildings under 50 years — over the remaining period of the lease.
Fixtures, fittings and equipment — $6\frac{2}{3}$ to $33\frac{1}{3}$ per cent according to the estimated life of the asset.

a Depreciation is not provided on freehold and long leasehold properties where, in the opinion of the directors, the residual values of those properties are such that any depreciation charge would be immaterial.

b Depreciation is charged on all additions to depreciating assets in the year of purchase.

Foreign currencies
The trading results of overseas subsidiaries have been translated using average rates of exchange ruling during the financial year.

The balance sheets of overseas subsidiaries have been translated into sterling at the rates of exchange ruling at 31 March, except for those assets and liabilities where a forward exchange contract has been arranged, in which case this forward rate is used. Exchange differences arising between the translation into sterling of the net assets of these subsidiaries at rates ruling at the beginning and end of the year are dealt with through reserves.

The cost of the Company's investment in overseas subsidiaries is translated at the rate ruling at the date of investment. All other foreign currency assets and liabilities of the Company and its United Kingdom subsidiaries are translated into sterling at the rate ruling at 31 March, except in those instances where a forward exchange contract has been arranged in which case this forward rate has been used. These exchange differences are dealt with through the profit and loss account.

Transactions during the year between the Company and its subsidiaries, customers and suppliers are translated into sterling at the rate of exchange ruling on the date of the transaction. All profits and losses on exchange realised during the year are dealt with through the profit and loss account.

Pension contributions
The Group operates pension schemes for the benefit of all its United Kingdom employees and for the majority of the staff overseas. The funds of the schemes are administered by Trustees and are separate from the Group. Independent actuaries complete valuations at least every three years. In accordance with their recommendations, annual contributions are paid to the schemes so as to

secure the benefits set out in the rules and to allow the periodic augmentation of current pensions. The cost of these and any variations from regular cost arising from actuarial valuations are charged or credited to profits on a systematic basis over the estimated remaining service lives of the employees.

Repairs and renewals

Expenditure on repairs, renewals and minor items of equipment is written off in the year in which it is incurred.

Stocks

Stocks and work in progress are valued at the lower of cost and net realisable value.

Retail stocks consist of goods for resale. Cost is computed by deducting the gross profit margin from the selling value of stock. When computing net realisable value an allowance is made for future markdowns.

The cost of work in progress comprises materials, labour and attributable overheads.

Trading results

The trading results include transactions at stores up to and including the nearest Saturday to 31 March. All other transactions are included up to 31 March in each year.

Scrip dividends

The amounts of dividends taken as shares instead of in cash under the scrip dividend schemes have been added back to reserves. The nominal value of shares issued under the scheme has been funded out of the share premium account.

NOTES TO THE FINANCIAL STATEMENTS

1   Trading period
The results for the year comprise store sales and related costs for the 52 weeks to 30 March 1991. All other activities are for the year to 31 March 1991.

2   Turnover
a Retailing
Turnover represents goods sold to customers outside the Group, less returns and sales taxes.

b Financial activities
Financial activities comprise financial services, treasury and insurance. Financial services include Chargecard, Budgetcard, personal loans and the management of unit trusts. Turnover represents the interest and other income attributable to these activities.

	1991 £m	1990 £m
c Analysis of turnover — by activity and geographical market.		
(i) Retailing		
United Kingdom and Republic of Ireland stores	**4,947·4**	4,765·4
Overseas stores:		
Continental Europe	**148·7**	119·9
North America (see below)	**508·1**	579·1
Far East	**20·1**	13·8
	676·9	712·8
Export sales outside the Group:		
Continental Europe	**47·3**	39·6
America	**2·9**	3·2
Africa	**1·3**	1·3
Far East	**7·5**	5·2
	59·0	49·3
	5,683·3	5,527·5
(ii) Financial activities	**91·5**	80·6
	5,774·8	5,608·1

The turnover attributable to financial activities arises wholly within the United Kingdom and the Channel Islands.
The turnover for North America of £508·1 million (last year £579·1 million) is analysed as follows:

USA		
Brooks Brothers (including Japan)	**163·2**	189·4
Kings Super Markets	**153·7**	179·0
	316·9	368·4
Canada		
Marks & Spencer division	**73·3**	79·7
Peoples	**81·4**	89·1
D'Allaird's	**36·5**	41·9
	191·2	210.7

3   Other expenses

The directors consider that the nature of the business is such that the analysis of expenses shown below is more informative than that set out in the formats in the Companies Act 1985.

	1991 £m	1990 £m
Other expenses comprise:		
Staff costs (see also note 10)	**716·4**	656·6
Occupancy costs	**196·0**	176·2
Other costs including Auditors' remuneration of £0·7 million (last year £0·6 million)	**200·8**	214·6
Repairs, renewals and maintenance of properties, fixtures, fittings and equipment	**43·4**	47·7
Depreciation of tangible fixed assets	**115·9**	109·4
Loss on sale of tangible fixed assets	**4·7**	7·4
	1,277·2	1,211·9
Other expenses include rentals under operating leases, comprising:		
— Hire of plant and machinery	**6·7**	7·0
— Other rental costs	**64·3**	62·7

4   Interest

	1991 £m	1990 £m
Bank and other interest receivable	**47·5**	33·6
Interest payable (see below)	**(34·2)**	(42·4)
	13·3	(8·8)
Interest payable by the Group comprises:		
Bank loans and overdrafts	**(13·9)**	(12·9)
Debenture loans — repayable within five years	**(0·7)**	(0·9)
Debenture loans — repayable in more than five years	**(2·3)**	(2·3)
9·75% Guaranteed loans 1993	**(21·2)**	(20·3)
8·25% Guaranteed bonds 1996	**(14·3)**	(13·8)
US$ Promissory note 1998	**(21·5)**	(26·1)
	(73·9)	(76·3)
Classified as:		
Interest payable	**(34·2)**	(42·4)
Cost of sales in the trading results of the financial activities	**(39·7)**	(33·9)
	(73·9)	(76·3)
Included as turnover in the trading results of the financial activities:		
Bank and other interest receivable	**80·2**	68·2

Income from listed investments during the year was £1·5 million (last year (0·6) million)

5   Exceptional charge

	1991 £m	1990 £m
Restructuring costs	**16·0**	—

The exceptional charge represents a provision for redundancy and associated costs mainly arising from the restructure of Head Office.

NOTES TO THE FINANCIAL STATEMENTS

6 Profit on ordinary activities before taxation	1991 £m	1990 £m
This arises as follows:		
United Kingdom and Republic of Ireland	**603·1**	597·6
Continental Europe	**20·4**	14·8
North America and Far East (see below)	**10·0**	15·3
Operating profit	**633·5**	627·7
Net interest receivable/(payable)	**13·3**	(8·8)
UK profit sharing	**(15·3)**	(14·7)
Exceptional charge (see note 5)	**(16·0)**	—
	615·5	604·2
and can be analysed between:		
Retailing	**597·5**	590·9
Financial activities	**18·0**	13·3
	615·5	604·2
Operating profits for North America and Far East comprise the following:		
USA		
Brooks Brothers (including Japan)	**5·9**	13·6
Kings Super Markets	**5·5**	7·0
Corporate expenses	**(1·1)**	(2·7)
	10·3	17·9
Canada		
Marks & Spencer division	**(4·7)**	(5·4)
Peoples	**0·5**	(1·5)
D'Allaird's	**1·3**	3·2
Corporate expenses	**(0·7)**	(0·9)
	(3·6)	**(4·6)**
Far East	**3·3**	2·0

7 Tax on profit on ordinary activities	1991 £m	1990 £m
The taxation charge comprises:		
Current taxation		
UK corporation tax at 34% (last year 35%)		
Current year	**210·8**	217·9
Prior years	**3·1**	(7·2)
	213·9	210·7
Double taxation relief	**(0·9)**	(3·2)
	213·0	207·5
Overseas tax	**10·8**	9·1
	223·8	216·6
Deferred taxation (see note 16)		
Current year	**(6·7)**	(3·6)
Prior years	**(1·3)**	1·5
	(8·0)	(2·1)
	215·8	214·5

8   Profit for the financial year

As permitted by Section 230 of the Companies Act 1985, the profit and loss account of the Company is not presented as part of these financial statements.

The consolidated profit of £397·3 million (last year £389·0 million) includes £393·5 million (last year 395·9 million) which is dealt with in the accounts of the Company.

9   Earnings per share

The calculation of earnings per ordinary share is based on earnings pre the exceptional charge of £407·9 million and earnings post the exceptional charge of £397·2 million (last year £388·9 million) after deducting minority interests and preference dividends, and on 2,707,317,102 ordinary shares (last year 2,686,319,239), being the weighted average number of shares in issue during the year ended 31 March 1991.

At 31 March 1991, directors, senior employees and retired staff held unexercised options in respect of 19,487,812 ordinary shares (last year 18,529,439). There were options outstanding under the Savings-Related Share Option Scheme in respect of 44,585,728 shares (last year 41,931,896). If all outstanding options had been exercised, the dilution of earnings per share would not have been material.

10   Directors and employees

a The number of directors of the Company performing their duties mainly within the United Kingdom whose emoluments (excluding pension contributions) were within the following ranges, are:

Gross Emoluments £	1991	1990	Gross Emoluments £	1991	1990	Gross Emoluments £	1991	1990
615,001 – 620,000	—	1	255,001 – 260,000	—	1	190,001 – 195,000	3	—
585,001 – 590,000	1	—	230,001 – 235,000	1	—	185,001 – 190,000	1	—
485,001 – 490,000	—	1	225,001 – 230,000	1	—	155,001 – 160,000	2	—
450,001 – 455,000	1	—	220,001 – 225,000	—	1	145,001 – 150,000	2	—
380,001 – 385,000	—	1	215,001 – 220,000	—	1	45,001 – 50,000	1	—
365,001 – 370,000	1	—	210,001 – 215,000	—	2	40,001 – 45,000	—	5
295,001 – 300,000	—	1	205,001 – 210,000	—	1	25,001 – 30,000	2	—
265,001 – 270,000	1	—	200,001 – 205,000	1	—	20,001 – 25,000	2	4

Included in the above is the remuneration of the Chairman during the year, The Lord Rayner, of £585,489 (last year £619,961). He was also the highest paid director.

Total directors' emoluments, including pension scheme contributions, were £4·4 million (last year £4·2 million). This includes a full year charge of £0·7 million in respect of the four directors appointed on 22 January 1990 (last year £0·2 million from date of appointment).

One director has waived the right to receive emoluments of £1,024 during the year.

The Group introduced an annual bonus scheme for executive directors and divisional directors in 1988 based on the achievement of certain profit targets. The remuneration committee has not approved the payment of a bonus this year. Last year the committee approved a bonus of £1·3 million of which £0·7 million was paid pro rata to each executive director's basic salary and is included in the total directors' emoluments for last year shown above. The remaining £0.6 million was paid to divisional directors last year.

10   **Directors and employees** continued

b The average weekly number of employees of the Group during the year was:

		1991	1990
UK Stores:	Management and supervisory categories	**5,878**	6,021
	Other	**50,745**	51,100
UK Head Office:	Management and supervisory categories	**2,250**	2,252
	Other	**2,057**	2,096
Financial Services:	Management and supervisory categories	**61**	54
	Other	**574**	542
Overseas		**12,693**	13,079
		74,258	75,144

If the number of part-time hours worked was converted on the basis of a full working week, the equivalent average number of full-time employees would have been 48,166 (last year 50,120).

The aggregate remuneration and associated costs of Group employees were:

	1991	1990
	£m	£m
Wages and salaries	**594·3**	553·7
Social security costs	**43·4**	38·7
Pension costs (see below)	**55·2**	47·1
Staff welfare and other personnel costs	**39·7**	37·5
	732·6	677·0
Classified as:		
Other expenses — staff costs	**716·4**	656·6
Manufacturing cost of sales	**16·2**	20·4
	732·6	677·0

11 Pension costs

The Group operates a number of funded defined benefit pension schemes throughout the world.

The assets of the schemes are held in separate trustee administered funds, and contributions are charged to the profit and loss account so as to spread the cost of pensions over employees' service lives with the Group. The pension cost relating to the UK scheme is assessed in accordance with the advice of an independent qualified actuary using the projected unit method, on the basis of triennial valuations.

The total pension cost for the Group was £55·2 million (last year £47·1 million) of which £5·4 million (last year £5·3 million) relates to the overseas schemes.

The latest actuarial valuation of the UK scheme was carried out at 1 April 1989. The assumptions which have the most significant effect on the results of the valuation are those relating to the rate of return on investments and the rate of increase in salaries. It was assumed that the investment return would be 10 per cent per annum and that future salary and wage increases would average 8 per cent per annum.

At the date of the last actuarial valuation, the market value of the assets of the UK scheme was £1,058·2 million and the actuarial valuation of these assets represented 107 per cent of the benefits that had accrued to members, after allowing for expected future increases in earnings. The surplus of the actuarial valuation of assets over the benefits accrued to members was £71·7 million. This is being spread over six years from 1 April 1989, being the remaining estimated service lives of the existing members, by a reduction in the annual contribution made to the scheme.

The pension costs relating to overseas schemes have been determined in accordance with the advice of independent qualified actuaries.

As shown in note 16 on page 52, the Company has pre-paid a contribution of £49·8 million to the UK scheme.

12 Share schemes

a Profit sharing:

The Trustees of the United Kingdom Employees' Profit Sharing Schemes have been allocated £15·3 million (last year £14·7 million) with which to subscribe for ordinary shares in the Company. The price of each share is 254·0p, being the average market price for the three dealing days immediately following the announcement of the results for the year ended 31 March 1991.

b United Kingdom Senior Staff Share Option Schemes:

Under the terms of the 1984 and 1987 schemes, following the announcement of the Company's results, the Board may offer options to purchase ordinary shares in the Company to directors and senior employees at the higher of the nominal value of the shares and the average market price for three consecutive dealing days preceding the date of the offer. The 1977 scheme has now expired and no further options may be granted under this scheme. Although options may be granted under both the 1984 and 1987 schemes, the maximum option value that can be exercised under each scheme is limited to four times earnings. Outstanding options granted under all senior schemes are as follows:

Options granted	Number of shares		Option price	Option dates
	1991	1990		
(1977 Scheme)				
May 1984	**27,422**	94,986	127·625p	May 1987–May 1991
May 1985	**832,427**	2,139,948	137·000p	May 1988–May 1992
May 1986	**778,878**	1,026,952	211·000p	May 1989–May 1993
May 1987	**1,188,686**	1,252,343	232·333p	May 1990–May 1994
(1984) Scheme)				
October 1984	**1,415,665**	2,288,070	115·667p	Oct 1987–Oct 1994
May 1985	**408,810**	1,304,433	137·000p	May 1988–May 1995
May 1986	**519,294**	952,481	211·000p	May 1989–May 1996
May 1987	**1,216,306**	1,248,973	232·333p	May 1990–May 1997
October 1987	**683,923**	917,539	202·000p	Oct 1990–Oct 1997
May 1988	**3,266,313**	3,377,174	176·000p	May 1991–May 1998
October 1988	**64,234**	64,234	158·000p	Oct 1991–Oct 1998
May 1989	**2,971,722**	3,048,787	175·000p	May 1992–May 1999
October 1989	**61,038**	61,038	188·000p	Oct 1992–Oct 1999
May 1990	**3,184,801**	—	206·000p	May 1993–May 2000
(1987 Scheme)				
October 1987	**735,811**	917,539	202·000p	Oct 1990–Oct 1994
May 1988	**6,412,682**	6,589,101	176·000p	May 1991–May 1995
October 1988	**64,234**	64,234	158·000p	Oct 1991–Oct 1995
May 1989	**3,195,184**	3,227,069	175·000p	May 1992–May 1996
October 1989	**61,038**	61,038	188·000p	Oct 1992–Oct 1996
May 1990	**4,030,566**	—	206·000p	May 1993–May 1997

No options were granted in October 1990.

c United Kingdom Employees' Savings-Related Share Option Scheme:

Under the terms of the scheme the Board may offer options to purchase ordinary shares in the Company once in each financial year to those employees who enter into an Inland Revenue approved Save As You Earn (SAYE) savings contract. The price at which options may be offered is 80 per cent of the market price for three consecutive dealing days preceding the date of offer. The options may normally be exercised during the period of six months after the completion of the SAYE contract, either five or seven years after entering the scheme.

NOTES TO THE FINANCIAL STATEMENTS

Outstanding options granted under this scheme are as follows: Options granted	Number of shares 1991	1990	Option price
January 1984	568,523	1,438,193	93·5p
January 1985	3,431,350	4,347,310	103·0p
January 1986	2,850,005	4,081,211	163·0p
January 1987	6,971,269	7,624,902	175·0p
January 1988	6,012,795	6,522,163	182·0p
January 1989	5,486,385	5,995,561	143·0p
January 1990	10,480,385	11,211,202	151·0p
January 1991	8,785,016	—	182·0p

13   Fixed assets — tangible assets

(a) The Group   Land and buildings

	Freehold £m	Long leasehold £m	Short leasehold £m	Total £m	Fixtures, fittings & equipment £m	Assets in the course of construc-tion £m	Total fixed assets £m
Cost or valuation							
At 1 April 1990	1,273·2	697·5	174·7	2,145·4	671·5	31·3	2,848·2
Additions	36·9	21·0	20·7	78·6	126·1	95·7	300·4
Transfers from assets in the course of construction	10·3	43·5	6·0	59·8	4·8	(64·6)	—
Transfers	—	(2·0)	2·0	—	—	—	—
Disposals	(16·0)	(1·6)	(7·7)	(25·3)	(77·4)	—	(102·7)
Differences on exchange	(4·0)	(0·5)	(4·1)	(8·6)	(5·5)	(0·6)	(14·7)
At 31 March 1991	**1,300·4**	**757·9**	**191·6**	**2,249·9**	**719·5**	**61·8**	**3,031·2**
At valuation	832·1	469·0	16·9	1,318,0	—	—	1,318·0
At cost	468·3	288·9	174·7	931,9	719·5	61·8	1,713·2
	1,300·4	**757·9**	**191·6**	**2,249·9**	**719·5**	**61·8**	**3,031·2**
Accumulated depreciation							
At 1 April 1990	5·8	1·6	44·1	51·5	328·2	—	379·7
Depreciation for the year	0·1	—	10·7	10·8	105·1	—	115·9
Disposals	(0·2)	—	(3·9)	(4·1)	(69·0)	—	(73·1)
Differences on exchange	(0·2)	—	(1·1)	(1·3)	(2·6)	—	(3·9)
At 31 March 1991	**5·5**	**1·6**	**49·8**	**56·9**	**361·7**	**—**	**418·6**
Net book value							
At 31 March 1991	**1,294·9**	**756·3**	**141·8**	**2·193·0**	**357·8**	**61·8**	**2,612·6**
At 31 March 1990	1,267·4	695·9	130·6	2,093·9	343·3	31·3	2,468·5

13   Fixed assets — tangible assets continued
(b) The Company

	Freehold £m	Long leasehold £m	Short leasehold £m	Total £m	Fixtures, fittings & equipment £m	Assets in the course of construc- tion £m	Total fixed assets £m
Cost or valuation							
At 1 April 1990	1,193·3	685·1	96·3	1,974·7	556·6	25·7	2,557·0
Additions	16·5	21·0	14·4	51·9	114·1	82·1	248·1
Transfers from assets in the course of construction	10·1	43·5	2·8	56.4	—	(56·4)	—
Transfers	—	(1·8)	1·8	—	—	—	—
Disposals	(14·7)	(1·6)	(2·8)	(19·1)	(68·5)	—	(87·6)
Differences on exchange	—	—	(0·2)	(0·2)	(0·1)	—	(0·3)
At 31 March 1991	**1,205·2**	**746·2**	**112·3**	**2,063·7**	**602·1**	**51·4**	**2,717·2**
At valuation	832·1	469·0	16·9	1,318·0	—		1,318·0
At cost	373·1	277·2	95·4	745·7	602·1	51·4	1,399·2
	1,205·2	**746·2**	**112·3**	**2,063·7**	**602·1**	**51·4**	**2,717·2**
Accumulated depreciation							
At 1 April 1990	2·4	1·6	12·1	16·1	263·8	—	279·9
Depreciation for the year	—	—	4·9	4·9	92·8	—	97·7
Disposals	—	—	(0·6)	(0·6)	(61·6)	—	(62·2)
At 31 March 1991	**2·4**	**1·6**	**16·4**	**20·4**	**295·0**	**—**	**315·4**
Net book value							
At 31 March 1991	**1,202·8**	**744·6**	**95·9**	**2·043·3**	**307·1**	**51·4**	**2,401·8**
At 31 March 1990	1,190·9	683·5	84·2	1,958·6	292·8	25·7	2,277·1

(i) Gerald Eve, chartered surveyors, valued the Company's freehold and leasehold properties in the United Kingdom and the Isle of Man as at 31 March 1982. This valuation was on the basis of open market value for existing use. At 31 March 1988, the directors, after consultation with Gerald Eve, revalued those of the Company's properties which had been valued as at 31 March 1982 (excluding subsequent additions and adjusted for disposals). The directors' valuation was incorporated into the financial statements at 31 March 1988.

(ii) If the Company's land and buildings had not been valued at 31 March 1982 and 31 March 1988 their net book value would have been:

	1991 £m	1990 £m
At valuation at 31 March 1975	351·9	358·7
At cost	983·4	874·4
At 31 March 1991	1.335·3	1.233·1
Accumulated depreciation	64·1	60·2
	1,271·2	1,172·9

The Company also valued its land and buildings in 1955 and in 1964. In the opinion of the directors unreasonable expense would be incurred in obtaining the original costs of the assets valued in those years and in 1975.

(iii) The Company does not maintain detailed records of cost and depreciation for fixtures, fittings and equipment. The accumulated cost figures represent reasonable estimates of the sums involved.

NOTES TO THE FINANCIAL STATEMENTS

14   Fixed assets — investments
The Company
a These investments comprise unlisted investments in and loans to subsidiaries.

	Shares in subsidiaries £m	Loans £m	Total £m
Cost			
At 1 April 1990	408·1	25·3	433·4
Additions	101·8	—	101·8
At 31 March 1991	**509·9**	**25·3**	**535·2**

b The Company's principal subsidiaries are set out below. A schedule of interests in all subsidiaries is filed with the Annual Return.

	Principal activity	Country of incorporation and operation	Proportion of ordinary shares held by:	
			The Company	A subsidiary
Marks and Spencer (Nederland) BV	Holding Company	The Netherlands	100%	—
Marks and Spencer (France) SA	Chain Store	France	—	100%
Marks and Spencer (Ireland) Limited	Chain Store	Ireland	—	100%
M&S Export (Ireland) Limited	Export	Ireland	—	100%
SA Marks and Spencer (Belgium) NV	Chain Store	Belgium	—	100%
M&S (Spain) SA	Holding Company	Spain	100%	—
Marks and Spencer (España) SA	Chain Store	Spain	—	67%
Marks & Spencer Holdings Canada Inc	Holding Company	Canada	—	100%
Marks & Spencer Canada Inc	Chain Store	Canada	—	100%
Marks and Spencer Finance (Nederland) BV	Finance	The Netherlands	—	100%
MS Insurance Limited	Insurance	Guernsey	—	100%
Marks and Spencer US Holdings Inc	Holding Company	United States	100%	—
Brooks Brothers Inc	Chain Store	United States	—	100%
Brooks Brothers, (Japan) Limited	Chain Store	Japan	—	51%
Kings Super Markets Inc	Chain Store	United States	—	100%
Marks & Spencer Services Inc	Management Services	United States	—	100%
Marks & Spencer Finance Inc	Finance	United States	—	100%
Marks and Spencer Retail Financial Services Holdings Limited	Holding Company	England	100%	—
Marks and Spencer Financial Services Limited	Finance	England	—	100%
Marks and Spencer Unit Trust Management Limited	Finance	England	—	100%
St Michael Finance Limited	Finance	England	100%	—
Marks and Spencer Property Holdings Limited	Property	England	100%	—
Marks and Spencer Property Developments Limited	Property Development	England	—	100%
Marks and Spencer Finance plc	Finance	England	100%	—
Marks and Spencer Export Corporation Limited	Management Services	England	100%	—

15   Stocks

	The Group		The Company	
	1991	1990	1991	1990
	£m	£m	£m	£m
Retail stocks	**343·5**	365·8	**235·8**	268·7
Work in progress	**1·9**	1·9	—	—
Raw materials	**5·7**	6·6	—	—
	351·1	374·3	**235·8**	268·7

16   Debtors

	The Group		The Company	
	1991	1990	1991	1990
	£m	£m	£m	£m
Amounts falling due within one year:				
Trade debtors and customer balances	**211·7**	192·1	**17·2**	19·4
Amounts owed by Group companies	—	—	**484·2**	472·2
Other debtors	**56·6**	51·1	**38·6**	37·2
Prepayments and accrued income	**85·4**	83·1	**74·2**	71·2
	353·7	326·3	**614·2**	600·0
Amounts falling due after more than one year:				
Advance corporation tax recoverable on the proposed final dividend	**42·5**	40·9	**42·5**	40·9
Deferred taxation provision arising on short-term timing differences	**(13·5)**	(21·6)	**(10·9)**	(18·4)
	29·0	19·3	**31·6**	22·5
Customer balances	**216·9**	174·1	—	—
Other debtors	**18·1**	17·9	**18·1**	17·8
	264·0	211·3	**49·7**	40·3
	617·7	537·6	**663·9**	640·3

Trade debtors include advances to suppliers of £5·2 million (last year £6·7 million) against bills of exchange drawn on the Company in respect of merchandise to be delivered between April and May 1991.

Other debtors include loans to employees, the majority of which are connected with house purchases. These include a loan to an officer of the Company, the balance of which amounted to £5,928 at 31 March 1991 (last year £8,112). Transactions with directors are set out in note 25 on page 56.

Prepayments and accrued income include £49·8 million in respect of the UK pension scheme for 1991/92 (last year £50·6 million in respect of 1990/91).

The decrease of £8·1 million (last year £1·5 million) in the Group's provision for deferred taxation is represented by a credit to the profit and loss account of £8·0 million (last year £2·1 million) and exchange movements of £0·1 million (last year £0·6 million).

NOTES TO THE FINANCIAL STATEMENTS

17 Current assets — investments

	The Group		The Company	
	1991	1990	1991	1990
	£m	£m	£m	£m
Investments listed on a recognised stock exchange:				
Government securities	**7·3**	8·8	—	4·9
Other	**6·5**	4·3	—	—
Certificates of tax deposit	**6·9**	14·2	**6·9**	14·2
Other	**8·1**	0·8	**5·5**	—
	28·8	28·1	**12·4**	19·1

The market value of the Group's government securities is £7·3 million (last year £8·6 million) and the market value of other listed investments is £6·5 million (last year £3·8 million).

The market value of the Company's government securities is nil (last year £4·9 million).

18 Cash at bank and in hand
Cash at bank includes short-term deposits with banks and other financial institutions.

19 Creditors: amounts falling due within one year

	The Group		The Company	
	1991	1990	1991	1990
	£m	£m	£m	£m
Debenture loan — secured				
5½% — 1985/1990	—	5·0	—	5·0
Bank loans, overdrafts and commercial paper	**100·0**	87·4	**3·2**	2·2
Trade creditors	**168·1**	186·6	**138·9**	149·7
Bills of exchange payable	**7·0**	7·4	**7·0**	7·4
Amounts owed to Group companies	—	—	**22·0**	15·2
Taxation	**228·0**	234·4	**218·8**	227·0
Social security and other taxes	**31·4**	25·7	**22·7**	19·9
Other creditors	**72·2**	106·9	**51·4**	94·2
Accruals and deferred income	**162·4**	149·0	**122·7**	108·0
Proposed final dividend	**127·6**	122·6	**127·6**	122·6
	896·7	925·0	**714·3**	751·2

20   Creditors: amounts falling due after more than one year

	The Group 1991 £m	The Group 1990 £m	The Company 1991 £m	The Company 1990 £m
Repayable between one and two years:				
9·75% Guaranteed notes 1993	**150·0**	—	—	—
Amounts owed to Group companies	—	—	**150·0**	—
Repayable between two and five years:				
Debenture loan — secured				
6½% — 1989/1994	**10·0**	10·0	**10·0**	10·0
9·75% Guaranteed notes 1993	—	150·0	—	—
Amounts owed to Group companies	—	—	—	150·0
Bank and other loans	—	0·6	—	—
Other creditors	**0·8**	1·5	—	—
Repayable in five years or more:				
Debenture loans — secured				
7¼% — 1993/1998	**15·0**	15·0	**15·0**	15·0
7¾ — 1995/2000	**15·0**	15·0	**15·0**	150·0
8·25% Guaranteed bonds 1996	**100·0**	100·0	—	—
US$ Promissory note 1998	**258·8**	273·1	—	—
Amounts owed to Group companies	—	—	**100·0**	100·0
	549·6	565·2	**290·0**	290·0

Debenture loans comprise first mortage debenture stocks which are secured on certain freehold and leasehold properties of the Company. The Company is entitled to redeem the whole or any part of each stock at par, at any time between the two dates shown above.

21   Provisions for liabilities and charges

	The Group £m	The Company £m
At 1 April 1990	4·3	—
Exchange movement	(0·3)	—
Utilised during the year	(0·9)	—
Provision for restructuring costs (see note 5)	16·0	16·0
At 31 March 1991	**19·1**	16·0

The provision utilised by the Group during the year relates to reorganisation costs incurred in US subsidiaries acquired in 1988/89.

22   Called up share capital

	The Company 1991 £m	The Company 1990 £m
Authorised:		
3,200,000,000 ordinary shares of 25p each	800·0	800·0
350,000 7·0% cumulative preference shares of £1 each	0·4	0·4
1,000,000 4·9% cumulative preference shares of £1 each	1·0	1·0
	801·4	801·4

22 Called up share capital continued

	The Company 1991 £m	1990 £m
Allotted, called up and fully paid:		
2,714,876,548 ordinary shares of 25p each (last year 2,694,767,329)	**678·7**	673·6
350,000 7·0% cumulative preference shares of £1 each	**0·4**	0·4
1,000,000 4·9% cumulative preference shares of £1 each	**1·0**	1·0
	680·1	675·0

14,535,613 ordinary shares being a nominal value of £3·7 million were allotted during the year under the terms of the Company's share schemes which are described in note 12. The aggregate consideration received was £24·4 million. Contingent rights to the allotment of shares are also described in note 12. In addition, 5.573,606 shares with a nominal value of £1·4 million were allotted to shareholders making an election for scrip dividends. The nominal value of £1·4 million in respect of scrip dividends was funded out of the share premium account.

23 Shareholders' funds

	The Group 1991 £m	1990 £m	The Company 1991 £m	1990 £m
Called up share capital (see note 22)	**680·1**	675·0	**680·1**	675·0
Reserves				
Share premium account:				
At 1 April 1990	**50·0**	34·7	**50·0**	34·7
Shares issued relating to scrip dividend	**(1·4)**	(1·7)	**(1·4)**	(1·7)
Movement during the year	**20·7**	17·0	**20·7**	17·0
At 31 March 1991	**69·3**	50·0	**69·3**	50·0
Revaluation reserve:				
At 1 April 1990	**458·0**	456·5	**479·4**	479·4
Realised during the year	**(8·6)**	—	**(8·6)**	—
Exchange movement	**10·3**	1·5	**—**	—
At 31 March 1991	**459·7**	458·0	**470·8**	479·4
Profit and loss account:				
At 1 April 1990	**991·6**	757·8	**1,426·4**	1,190·1
Negative goodwill arising	**—**	1·7	**—**	—
Amounts added back in respect of scrip dividends	**12·5**	12·6	**12·5**	12·6
Undistributed surplus for the year	**215·3**	216·5	**211·5**	223·4
Exchange movement	**(1·1)**	3·0	**(0·4)**	0·3
At 31 March 1991	**1,218·3**	991·6	**1,650·0**	1,426·4
Shareholders' funds	**2,427·4**	2,174·6	**2,870·2**	2,630·8

For dividend payments made during this financial year, £9·2 million of the 1989/90 final dividend and £3·3 million of the 1990/91 interim dividend were paid by way of shares, and have been added to reserves (see above).

Cumulative goodwill of £478·9 million (last year £478·9 million) arising on the acquisition of US, Canadian and Spanish subsidiaries has been written off against the profit and loss account reserve in the years of acquisition.

24   Commitments and contingent liabilities

	The Group		The Company	
	1991 £m	1990 £m	1991 £m	1990 £m
a Commitments in respect of properties in the course of development	105·0	84·1	87·9	81·4
b Capital expenditure authorised by the directors but not yet contracted	400·1	498·4	358·3	492·1
c Deferred taxation not provided on the excess of capital allowances over depreciation on tangible assets	134·0	134·3	129·2	129·6
d Guarantees by the Company in respect of the Eurobonds and Promissory note issued by subsidiaries	—	—	508·8	523·1
e Guarantees by the Company of the Commercial Paper issued by St Michael Finance Limited	—	—	42·3	24·7
f Guarantees by the Company of the liabilities of Marks and Spencer (Nederland) BV, Marks and Spencer (Stores) BV, Marks and Spencer (Ireland) Limited and M&S Export (Ireland) Limited	—	—	14·1	11·6

Marks and Spencer (Ireland) Limited and M & S Export (Ireland) Limited have availed themselves of the exemption provided for in s17 of the Companies (Amendment) Act 1986 (Ireland) in respect of the documents required to be annexed to the annual returns of these companies.

g In the opinion of the directors, the revalued properties will be retained for use in the business and the likelihood of any taxation liability arising is remote. Accordingly the potential deferred taxation in respect of these properties has not been quantified.

h Other material contracts

In the event of a change in the trading arrangements with certain warehouse operators, the Company has a commitment to purchase, at market value, fixed assets which are currently owned and operated by them on the Company's behalf.

i Commitments under operating leases

At 31 March 1991 annual commitments under non-cancellable operating leases were as follows:

	The Group		The Company	
	Land and buildings £m	Other £m	Land and buildings £m	Other £m
Expiring within one year	2·0	0·4	—	0·1
Expiring between two and five years	14·8	4·5	0·8	3·9
Expiring in five years or more	51·0	—	30·7	—
	67·8	4·9	31·5	4·0

25   Transactions with directors

Interest-free house purchase loans were made under the employees' loan scheme, by the Company to the following, prior to his appointment as a director:

	Date of loan	At 31 March 1991 £	At 31 March 1990 £
Mr A Z Stone	1980–1989	26,000	46,500

The loan outstanding is to be repaid in the next financial year.

NOTES TO THE FINANCIAL STATEMENTS

26   Directors' interests in shares and debentures

The beneficial interests of the directors and their families in the shares of the Company and its subsidiaries, together with their interests as trustees of both charitable and other trusts, are shown below. Further information regarding employee share options is given in note 12 on pages 48 and 49.

Interests in the Company

Ordinary shares — beneficial and family interests

	At 31 March 1991		At 1 April 1990	
	Shares	Options	Shares	Options
The Lord Rayner	81,451	1,417,579	113,851	1,167,182
R Greenbury	44,311	1,012,236	37,525	1,012,713
C V Silver	40,904	917,387	34,983	746,997
N L Colne	61,725	676,560	82,245	590,402
R W C Colvill	10,285	379,783	4,451	281,743
J A Lusher	24,323	563,019	78,901	664,778
P G McCracken	7,658	248,460	6,394	244,589
J K Oates	13,990	704,800	10,068	910,690
A S Orton	21,142	678,720	17,335	547,918
S J Sacher	396,150	463,549	392,939	615,506
P L Salsbury	16,307	414,215	25,181	328,805
The Hon David Sieff	292,913	684,352	303,793	640,812
A K P Smith	183,299	881,353	226,716	754,702
A Z Stone	8,628	283,657	7,503	194,472
D G Trangmar	34,134	437,286	29,845	636,332
Dr D V Atterton CBE	4,204	—	4,120	—
R A E Herbert	7,990	8,344	7,482	8,344
D G Lanigan	2,631	6,181	2,060	—
D R Susman	57,386	—	55,823	—
The Rt Hon The Baroness Young DL	2,508	—	2,000	—

Ordinary shares — trustees' interests

	At 31 March 1991		At 1 April 1990	
	Charitable Trusts Shares	Other Trusts Shares	Charitable Trusts Shares	Other Trusts Shares
S J Sacher	396,690	171,368	391,690	206,748
The Hon David Sieff	30,000	67,242	218,532	546,064
D R Susman	570,100	—	570,100	—

Preference shares and debentures

At 31 March 1991 N L Colne owned 500 4·9 per cent preference shares (last year 500 shares). None of the other directors had an interest in any preference shares or in the debentures of the Company.

Interests in subsidiaries

None of the directors had any interests in any subsidiaries at the beginning or end of the year. Between the end of the financial year and one month prior to the date of the Notice of Meeting, there have been no changes in the directors' interests in shares and debentures of, and in options granted by, the Company and its subsidiaries.

Reproduced with the kind permission of Marks & Spencer, plc.

RATIO ANALYSIS OF MARKS AND SPENCER plc

The following ratios may be calculated for Marks and Spencer plc and used to assess its performance and for comparison with that of similar organizations.

1990
1991

1 *Gross profit to net capital employed*

$$\frac{\text{Gross profit} \times 100}{\text{Net capital employed}} = \frac{1839.6 \times 100}{2750.1} = 66.9\% \qquad\qquad \frac{1910.7 \times 100}{3006.5} = 63.6\%$$

2 *Net profit to net capital employed*

$$\frac{\text{Net profit} \times 100}{\text{Net capital employed}} = \frac{618.9 \times 100}{2750.1} = 22.5\% \qquad\qquad \frac{646.8 \times 100}{3006.5} = 21.5\%$$

3 *Gross profit on sales (Gross margin)*

$$\frac{\text{Gross profit} \times 100}{\text{Sales}} = \frac{1839.6 \times 100}{5608.1} = 32.8\% \qquad\qquad \frac{1910.7 \times 100}{5774.8} = 33.1\%$$

4 *Net profit on sales (Net margin)*

$$\frac{\text{Net profit} \times 100}{\text{Sales}} = \frac{618.9 \times 100}{5608.1} = 11\% \qquad\qquad \frac{646.8 \times 100}{5774.8} = 11.2\%$$

5 *Current ratio*

Current assets : current liabilities

$$1206.6 : 925.0 \qquad = 1.3:1 \qquad\qquad 1290.6 : 896.7 = 1.4 : 1$$

6 *Quick ratio (Acid test)*

Quick assets : current liabilities

$$832.3 : 925.0 \qquad = 0.9 : 1 \qquad\qquad 939.5 : 896.7 = 1.04 : 1$$

7 *Capital gearing ratio*

$$\frac{\text{Equity capital}}{\text{Fixed interest borrowing (note 20)}}$$

$$\frac{2174.6}{565.2} = 1 : 3.8 \text{ or } 26\% \qquad\qquad \frac{2427.4}{549.6} = 1 : 4.4 \text{ or } 22.6\%$$

8 *Times interest earned*

$$\frac{\text{Profit before fixed interest charges}}{\text{Fixed interest charges (note 4)}} = \frac{627.7}{42.4} = 14.8 \text{ times} \qquad\qquad \frac{633.5}{34.2} = 18.5 \text{ times}$$

9 *Debtors' ratio*

$$\frac{\text{Debtors (note 16)}}{\text{Average daily credit sales (note 2(i))}} = \frac{192.1}{15.35} = 12.5 \text{ days} \qquad\qquad \frac{211.7}{15.79} = 13.4 \text{ days}$$

Is this a realistic ratio for this organization?

	1990	1991

10 *Creditors' ratio*

$$\frac{\text{Creditors (note 19)}}{\text{Average daily credit purchases}} = \frac{186.6}{10.47} = 17.8 \text{ days} \qquad \frac{168.1}{10.73} = 15.7 \text{ days}$$

(no information on purchases, so approximate with "cost of sales")

Is this a useful ratio with the available information?

11 *Stock turnover*

$$\frac{\text{Cost of goods sold}}{\text{Average stock of finished goods (note 15)}} =$$

$$\frac{3768.5}{365.8} = 10.3 \text{ times pa} \qquad \frac{3864.1}{\left(\dfrac{365.8 + 343.5}{2}\right)}$$

$$= 35 \text{ days} \qquad = 11 \text{ times pa} = 32.7 \text{ days}$$

(Year end stock only is available for 1990)

12 *Fixed asset turnover*

$$\frac{\text{Sales}}{\text{Fixed assets}} = \frac{5608.1}{2468.5} = 2.3 \text{ times} \qquad \frac{5774.8}{2612.6} = 2.2 \text{ times}$$

Marks and Spencer is a highly successful organization. How do you feel the ratios which have been calculated could be applied to other businesses? Would the results be the same?

GLOSSARY

Accounting period Normally 12 months as far as the financial accounts are concerned, to coincide with the tax year. So far as the management accounts are concerned it can be any period ranging from one week to one year. It is generally thought necessary to provide management information at least once every four weeks.

Acid test Test of the ability of an organization to pay its way in the short term, given by the ratio of quick assets to current liabilities.

Activity based costing Allocation of costs on the basis of the use a product makes of a service.

Articles of association Internal rules that state the rights and duties of directors and shareholders of a company.

Assets Items belonging to the organization that have either a long-term or short-term value. Those having a long-term value are items like machinery and plant. They are called fixed assets.

Authorized capital The total amount of money that the organization is authorized to raise by the issue of share capital. The authorized capital is subject to stamp duty and so organizations do not state high authorized capital figures when they are first formed. The authorized share capital is not set for all time and can be varied if necessary.

Bit A binary digit (i.e. a 0 or 1).

Book value The value at which an asset is shown in the balance sheet.

Budget A budget is a forecast or estimate of the events over a stated future interval of time, e.g., one year, five years or five months.

Byte A group of bits. Normally 8 bits form a byte. Approximately 1000 bytes form a kilo-byte. Approximately 1000 kilo-bytes form a megabyte.

Capital employed The total of the assets owned. The net capital employed is more usually used in calculating ratios and is the total assets less the current liabilities.

Capital items Items that last for several years. Examples are machinery used in manufacture, motor vehicles, land and buildings.

Credit terms Providing or receiving goods or services for which payment will be made at a later date.

Current assets   Assets that are normally used up in one financial period and change from day to day.

Current liabilities   Liabilities that must be settled within a short time: they fluctuate from day to day.

Current ratio   Measure of the organization's ability to pay its way in the period between about three and nine months in the future. Given by the ratio of current assets to current liabilities.

Database   A common pool of structured data.

Database Management System (DBMS)   A set of programs that manage the access and integrity of a database.

Debenture   A certificate issued by a company acknowledging a debt.

Depreciation   Method of allocating the cost of a fixed asset over its useful life.

Differential costs   Costs that are altered by the suggested action.

Discounted cash flow   Future cash flows discounted to give their present value.

Dividend   Distribution of profits to the shareholders. Usually expressed as a dividend of xp in the £ on the nominal value of their shares.

Dividend cover   The number of times the earnings cover the declared dividend.

Earnings   Moneys received or due for goods or services provided by the organization.

Earnings per share   The profits available to be distributed divided by the number of shares.

Equity   The equity of the business is the part that belongs to the owners. What remains after all outside interests have received their money.

Expenses   Moneys paid or due to be paid by the organization for revenue goods or services it has received.

Expert system   A type of computer system that attempts to simulate the decisions and knowledge of a human expert in a given area.

Fixed assets   Assets held for many years to earn profits. Examples are land and buildings and plant and machinery.

Fixed cost   Cost that is incurred as a result of management policy and does not vary with the activity level. Examples are salaries, rates, depreciation.

Fixed overheads   Expenses that do not vary with the level of activity.

Floppy disk   Small transportable disks used for storing computer data. Original floppies were about 8 inch in diameter and of a flexible plastic material making them 'floppy'. Although disks have now decreased in size ($3\frac{1}{2}$-inch disks are fast becoming the standard) and are now fairly rigid, the term floppy has tended to stick.

Font   A set of characters set in a particular style, e.g. Gothic, Roman.

Gearing   Relationship between the share capital and loan capital of a business.

Goodwill   The excess over the book value of a business that is received when sold.

Hardware   The physical components of the computer.

Historical cost   The cost at which the assets were obtained.

Income statement   Used to calculate the profit or loss of an organization in an accounting period. Made up of
  1. *Manufacturing account* showing the costs of goods made.
  2. *Trading account* showing the gross profit or loss; the difference between the cost price and selling price of the goods.
  3. *Profit and loss account* showing the net profit or loss.

Insolvency   Failure to meet financial obligations.

Inventory   Stock.

Issued capital   The shares that have been issued by the organization in order to raise money.

Job cost   Cost of a single job or operation.

Just in time   Method of stock control under which the supplier acts as the stock holder and delivers supplies so that they can go straight to the production line.

LAN (Local Area Network)   Communications equipment (including both communications hardware and software) that links together computer equipment in a small geographical area.

Laser printer   A printer which uses laser light technology to print computer output on paper. Laser printers offer exceptionally good quality print and are useful for a variety of applications including wordprocessing, graphics and Desk Top Publishing.

Liabilities   Moneys that the organization owes.

Lightpen   A computer input device that reads normally coded data or instructions into computer memory.

Long-term liabilities   Long-term debts.

Marginal cost   The cost of one more.

Margin of safety   The excess of sales over the break-even point.

Mark-up   The percentage added to the cost price of goods to arrive at the selling price.

Market value of share   Price that the share would realize if sold.

Memorandum of association   Constitution of the company.

MODEM (Modulator-Demodulator)   A piece of equipment that converts electronic signals from a computer into a form suitable for transmission through telecommunications equipment.

Mouse   A computer input device, normally about the same size, colour, and shape of a common field mouse. Its rolling movement on a flat surface corresponds to the movement of the cursor on the computer screen.

Net assets   Total assets less current liabilities.

Net capital employed   The resources that are employed in the business for more than one year; enables the return on the long-term investment to be found. The net capital employed is calculated by deducting the current liabilities from the total assets.

Nominal value   Face value of a share.

Off balance sheet finance   Finance that is not fully recorded on the balance sheet, but often hidden as investment in subsidiary companies.

Operating system   A set of programs that act as the interface between the hardware and the application software.

Ordinary shares   Share capital that is not entitled to a fixed rate of dividend.

Personal computer (PC)   A computer designed for the use of only one person at any given time. The first PCs appeared in the mid-1970s and were a dramatic departure from existing computers where a number of devices/terminals had shared a single central processor. Now one central processor supported only one terminal. The credit for the first PCs goes to Apple Computers, but the market for PCs really took off when IBM introduced their PC in 1981.

Pitch   The number of characters capable of being printed in a given space, e.g. 10 characters per inch (cpi).

Preference shares   Share capital that has a fixed rate of dividend and receives its dividends before the rest of the share capital.

Prime costs   Direct materials, direct labour and direct expenses added together.

Profit   Surplus of earnings over expenses.

Public limited company (plc) Limited company that conforms to Common Market regulations.

Quick assets Those that are quickly and easily realizable—normally debtors and cash.

Quick ratio Acid test.

Reserves Profits that are retained in the business—rarely cash.

Retained profits Reserves.

Revenue items Items that are completely used up or discharged in one year. Examples are salaries, wages, heating, raw materials.

Revenue reserves Distributable to shareholders.

Share capital The amount received from the shareholders of the business.

Share premium A capital reserve (one which cannot be distributed to the shareholders) created when the company sells its shares at a price in excess of the nominal value.

Software The set of programs that instruct the hardware which actions to take.

Spreadsheet A piece of software which appears as a matrix of interrelated cells and which is capable of performing mathematical computations.

Standard cost Predetermined or expected cost.

Stock turnover Number of times the stock is turned over in a financial period, given by the ratio of cost of goods sold to cost of stock.

Turnover Total sales value.

Variable overheads Indirect expenses that vary with activity level.

Variances Differences between standard and actual performance.

WAN (Wide Area Network) Communications equipment that links together computer equipment over distinct geographical boundaries.

Winchester Disk A hard disk storage device developed especially for PCs. The disk drive, storage arms and read/write heads are held within a sealed unit. Winchester disks typically hold 20, 40, or 80 mega bytes of data.

Working capital Capital needed to keep the business operating until more money is obtained from operations. It is current assets minus current liabilities.

BIBLIOGRAPHY

Andrews, V. L., and P. Hunt, *Financial Management Cases and Readings*, Irwin, Homewood, Illinois, 1976. Revised edition.

Anthony, R. N., and J. Dierdon, *Management Control Systems*, Irwin, Homewood, Illinois, 1980. 4th edition.

Bierman, H., and S. Smidt, *The Capital Budgeting Decision*, Macmillan, New York: Collier, Macmillan, London, 1980. 5th edition.

Bromwich, M., *The Economics of Capital Budgeting*, Penguin, Harmondsworth, Middlesex, 1978. 2nd reprint.

Bull, R. J., *Accounting in Business*, Butterworths, London, 1980. 4th edition.

Carsberg, B. V., and A. Hope, *Business Investment Decisions Under Inflation*, Institute of Chartered Accountants, London, 1976.

Clarkson, C. P. E., and B. J. Elliott, *Managing Money and Finance*, Gower, Aldershot, 1983.

Emmanuel, C. R., T. Oltey and K. A. Merchant, *Accounting for Management Control*, Chapman and Hall, London, 1990, 2nd edition.

Glautier, M. W. E., and B. Underdown, *Accounting Theory and Practice*, Pitman, London, 1982. 2nd edition.

Goch, D., *Finance and Accounts for Managers*, Pan, London, 1980. Revised edition.

Hartley, W. C. F., *Introduction to Business Accounting for Managers*, Pergamon, Oxford, 1980. 3rd edition.

Hindmarch, A., M. Atchison, and R. Marke, *Accounting: An Introduction*, Macmillan, London and Basingstoke, 1977. 1st edition.

Horngren, C. T., *Cost Accounting—A Managerial Emphasis*, Prentice-Hall, London, 1982, 5th edition.

Hunt, P., C. N. Williams, and G. Donaldson, *Basic Business Finance Text*, Irwin, Homewood, Illinois, 1961. Revised edition.

Hyde, W., *Interim Guidelines on Inflation Accounting,* Accounting Standards Committee, 1977.

Lauderback, J. G., and M. L. Hirsch, *Cost Accounting*, Kent, Boston, Mass., 1982.

Merrett, A. J., and A. Sykes, *The Finance and Analysis of Capital Projects*, Longman, London, 1973. 2nd edition.

Miller, M. H., and F. Modigliani, *Dividend Policy, Growth and the Valuation of Shares*, in *Journal of Business*, Vol. 34, 1961, pages 411–433.

185

Newbould, G. D., *Business Finance*, Harrap, London, 1970.

Pile, R. and R. Dobbins, *Investment Decisions and Financial Strategy*, Philip Allan, Hemel Hempstead, 1986.

Puxty, A. G. and C. J. Dodds, *Financial Management and Meaning*, Chapman and Hall, London, 1991, 2nd edition.

Samuels, J. M., F. M. Wilkes and R. E. Brayshaw, *Management of Company Finance*, Chapman and Hall, London, 1990, 5th edition.

Siegel, G. and H. Ramanaushas-Marconi, *Behavioral Accounting*, Chapman and Hall, London, 1989.

Sizer, J., *An Insight into Management Accounting*, Pitman, London, 1979, 2nd edition.

Taylor, A. H., and R. E. Palmer, *Financial Planning for Managers*, Pan, London, 1980, Revised edition.

Van Horne, J. C., *Financial Management and Policy*, Prentice-Hall, London, 1983. 6th edition.

Van Horne, J. C., *Fundamentals of Financial Management*, Prentice-Hall International, London, 1986.

Watts, M., *Element of Finance for Managers*, Macdonald & Evans, Plymouth, 1976.

Wert, J. E., and C. L. Prather, *Financing Business Firms*, Irwin, Homewood, Illinois, 1975. 5th edition.

Weston, J. F., and E. F. Brigham, *Managerial Finance*, Holt, Rinehart & Winston, London, 1978. 6th edition.

Wilson, R. M. S., *Financial Control—A Systems Approach*, McGraw-Hill, London, 1974.

Wright, M. G., *Discounted Cash Flow*, McGraw-Hill, London, 1973. 2nd edition.

Wright, M. G., *Financial Management*, McGraw-Hill, Maidenhead, 1970.

Year	Amount to which £1 will accumulate	Present value of £1	Present value of £1 received at end of period	Present value of £1 received continuously	Amount received at end of year which will recover initial investment of £1	Amount received at end of year which will recover initial investment of £1	Year
1	1.0100	0.9901	0.9901	0.9950	1.0100	1.0050	1
2	1.0201	0.9803	1.9704	1.9802	0.5075	0.5050	2
3	1.0303	0.9706	2.9410	2.9557	0.3400	0.3383	3
4	1.0406	0.9610	3.9020	3.9214	0.2563	0.2550	4
5	1.0510	0.9515	4.8534	4.8777	0.2060	0.2050	5
6	1.0615	0.9420	5.7955	5.8244	0.1725	0.1717	6
7	1.0721	0.9327	6.7282	6.7618	0.1486	0.1479	7
8	1.0829	0.9235	7.6517	7.6899	0.1307	0.1300	8
9	1.0937	0.9143	8.5660	8.6088	0.1167	0.1162	9
10	1.1046	0.9053	9.4713	9.5186	0.1056	0.1051	10
11	1.1157	0.8963	10.3676	10.4194	0.0965	0.0960	11
12	1.1268	0.8874	11.2551	11.3113	0.0888	0.0884	12
13	1.1381	0.8787	12.1337	12.1943	0.0824	0.0820	13
14	1.1495	0.8700	13.0037	13.0686	0.0769	0.0765	14
15	1.1610	0.8613	13.8651	13.9343	0.0721	0.0718	15
16	1.1726	0.8528	14.7179	14.7913	0.0679	0.0676	16
17	1.1843	0.8444	15.5623	15.6399	0.0643	0.0639	17
18	1.1961	0.8360	16.3983	16.4801	0.0610	0.0607	18
19	1.2081	0.8277	17.2260	17.3120	0.0581	0.0578	19
20	1.2202	0.8195	18.0456	18.1356	0.0554	0.0551	20
21	1.2324	0.8114	18.8570	18.9511	0.0530	0.0528	21
22	1.2447	0.8034	19.6604	19.7585	0.0509	0.0506	22
23	1.2572	0.7954	20.4558	20.5579	0.0489	0.0486	23
24	1.2697	0.7876	21.2434	21.3494	0.0471	0.0468	24
25	1.2824	0.7798	22.0232	22.1331	0.0454	0.0452	25
1	1.0200	0.9804	0.9804	0.9902	1.0200	1.0099	1
2	1.0404	0.9612	1.9416	1.9609	0.5150	0.5100	2
3	1.0612	0.9423	2.8839	2.9126	0.3468	0.3433	3
4	1.0824	0.9238	3.8077	3.8457	0.2626	0.2600	4
5	1.1041	0.9057	4.7135	4.7604	0.2122	0.2101	5
6	1.1262	0.8880	5.6014	5.6573	0.1785	0.1768	6
7	1.1487	0.8706	6.4720	6.5365	0.1545	0.1530	7
8	1.1717	0.8535	7.3255	7.3985	0.1365	0.1352	8
9	1.1951	0.8368	8.1622	8.2436	0.1225	0.1213	9
10	1.2190	0.8203	8.9826	9.0721	0.1113	0.1102	10
11	1.2434	0.8043	9.7868	9.8844	0.1022	0.1012	11
12	1.2682	0.7885	10.5753	10.6807	0.0946	0.0936	12
13	1.2936	0.7730	11.3484	11.4615	0.0881	0.0872	13
14	1.3195	0.7579	12.1062	12.2269	0.0826	0.0818	14
15	1.3459	0.7430	12.8493	12.9773	0.0778	0.0771	15
16	1.3728	0.7284	13.5777	13.7130	0.0737	0.0729	16
17	1.4002	0.7142	14.2919	14.4343	0.0700	0.0693	17
18	1.4282	0.7002	14.9920	15.1415	0.0667	0.0660	18
19	1.4568	0.6864	15.6785	15.8347	0.0638	0.0632	19
20	1.4859	0.6730	16.3514	16.5144	0.0612	0.0606	20
21	1.5157	0.6598	17.0112	17.1808	0.0588	0.0582	21
22	1.5460	0.6468	17.6580	17.8340	0.0566	0.0561	22
23	1.5769	0.6342	18.2922	18.4745	0.0547	0.0541	23
24	1.6084	0.6217	18.9139	19.1024	0.0529	0.0523	24
25	1.6406	0.6095	19.5235	19.7180	0.0512	0.0507	25

1.0% (years 1–25, first block)

2.0% (years 1–25, second block)

	Year	Amount to which £1 will accumulate	Present value of £1	Present value of £1 received at end of period	Present value of £1 received continuously	Amount received at end of year which will recover initial investment of £1	Amount received at end of year which will recover initial investment of £1	Year	
	1	1.0300	0.9709	0.9709	0.9854	1.0300	1.0149	1	
	2	1.0609	0.9426	1.9135	1.9420	0.5226	0.5149	2	
	3	1.0927	0.9151	2.8286	2.8708	0.3535	0.3483	3	
	4	1.1255	0.8885	3.7171	3.7726	0.2690	0.2651	4	
	5	1.1593	0.8626	4.5797	4.6481	0.2184	0.2151	5	
	6	1.1941	0.8375	5.4172	5.4980	0.1846	0.1819	6	
	7	1.2299	0.8131	6.2303	6.3233	0.1605	0.1581	7	
	8	1.2668	0.7894	7.0197	7.1245	0.1425	0.1404	8	
	9	1.3048	0.7664	7.7861	7.9023	0.1284	0.1265	9	
	10	1.3439	0.7441	8.5302	8.6575	0.1172	0.1155	10	
	11	1.3842	0.7224	9.2526	9.3907	0.1081	0.1065	11	
3.0%	12	1.4258	0.7014	9.9540	10.1026	0.1005	0.0990	12	3.0%
	13	1.4685	0.6810	10.6350	10.7937	0.0940	0.0926	13	
	14	1.5126	0.6611	11.2961	11.4647	0.0855	0.0872	14	
	15	1.5580	0.6419	11.9379	12.1161	0.0838	0.0825	15	
	16	1.6047	0.6232	12.5611	12.7486	0.0796	0.0784	16	
	17	1.6528	0.6050	13.1661	13.3626	0.0760	0.0748	17	
	18	1.7024	0.5874	13.7535	13.9588	0.0727	0.0716	18	
	19	1.7535	0.5703	14.3238	14.5376	0.0698	0.0688	19	
	20	1.8061	0.5537	14.8775	15.0995	0.0672	0.0662	20	
	21	1.8063	0.5375	15.4150	15.6451	0.0649	0.0639	21	
	22	1.9161	0.5219	15.9369	16.1748	0.0627	0.0618	22	
	23	1.9736	0.5067	16.4436	16.6890	0.0608	0.0599	23	
	24	2.0328	0.4919	16.9355	17.1883	0.0590	0.0582	24	
	25	2.0938	0.4776	17.4131	17.6731	0.0574	0.0566	25	
	1	1.0400	0.9615	0.9615	0.9806	1.0400	1.0197	1	
	2	1.0816	0.9246	1.8861	1.9236	0.5302	0.5199	2	
	3	1.1249	0.8890	2.7751	2.8302	0.3603	0.3533	3	
	4	1.1699	0.8548	3.6299	3.7020	0.2755	0.2701	4	
	5	1.2167	0.8219	4.4518	4.5403	0.2246	0.2203	5	
	6	1.2653	0.7903	5.2421	5.3463	0.1908	0.1870	6	
	7	1.3169	0.7599	6.0021	6.1213	0.1666	0.1634	7	
	8	1.3686	0.7307	6.7327	6.8665	0.1485	0.1456	8	
	9	1.4233	0.7026	7.4353	7.5831	0.1345	0.1319	9	
	10	1.4802	0.6756	8.1109	8.2721	0.1233	0.1209	10	
	11	1.5395	0.6496	8.7605	8.9345	0.1141	0.1119	11	
4.0%	12	1.6010	0.6246	9.3851	9.5715	0.1066	0.1045	12	4.0%
	13	1.6651	0.6006	9.9856	10.1841	0.1001	0.0982	13	
	14	1.7317	0.5775	10.5631	10.7730	0.0947	0.0928	14	
	15	1.8009	0.5553	11.1184	11.3393	0.0899	0.0882	15	
	16	1.8730	0.5339	11.6523	11.8838	0.0858	0.0841	16	
	17	1.9479	0.5134	12.1657	12.4074	0.0822	0.0806	17	
	18	2.0258	0.4936	12.6593	12.9108	0.0790	0.0775	18	
	19	2.1068	0.4746	13.1339	13.3949	0.0761	0.0747	19	
	20	2.1911	0.4564	13.5903	13.8604	0.0736	0.0721	20	
	21	2.2788	0.4388	14.0292	14.3079	0.0713	0.0699	21	
	22	2.3699	0.4220	14.4511	14.7382	0.0692	0.0679	22	
	23	2.4647	0.4057	14.8568	15.1520	0.0673	0.0660	23	
	24	2.5633	0.3901	15.2470	15.5499	0.0656	0.0643	24	
	25	2.6658	0.3751	15.6221	15.9325	0.0640	0.0628	25	

	Year	Amount to which £1 will accumulate	Present value of £1	Present value of £1 received at end of period	Present value of £1 received continuously	Amount received at end of year which will recover initial investment of £1	Amount received at end of year which will recover initial investment of £1	Year	
	1	1.0500	0.9524	0.9524	0.9760	1.0500	1.0246	1	
	2	1.1025	0.9070	1.8594	1.9055	0.5378	0.5248	2	
	3	1.1576	0.8638	2.7232	2.7908	0.3672	0.3583	3	
	4	1.2155	0.8227	3.5460	3.6399	0.2820	0.2752	4	
	5	1.2763	0.7835	4.3295	4.4368	0.2310	0.2254	5	
	6	1.3401	0.7462	5.0757	5.2016	0.1970	0.1923	6	
	7	1.4071	0.7107	5.7864	5.9299	0.1728	0.1686	7	
	8	1.4775	0.6768	6.4632	6.6235	0.1547	0.1510	8	
	9	1.5513	0.6446	7.1078	7.2841	0.1407	0.1373	9	
	10	1.6289	0.6139	7.7217	7.9132	0.1295	0.1264	10	
	11	1.7103	0.5847	8.3064	8.5124	0.1204	0.1175	11	
5.0%	12	1.7959	0.5568	8.8633	9.0830	0.1128	0.1101	12	5.0%
	13	1.8856	0.5303	9.3936	9.6263	0.1065	0.1039	13	
	14	1.9799	0.5051	9.8986	10.1441	0.1010	0.0986	14	
	15	2.0789	0.4810	10.3797	10.6370	0.0963	0.0940	15	
	16	2.1829	0.4581	10.8378	11.1065	0.0923	0.0900	16	
	17	2.2920	0.4363	11.2741	11.5536	0.887	0.0866	17	
	18	2.4066	0.4155	11.6896	11.9795	0.0855	0.0835	18	
	19	2.5270	0.3957	12.0853	12.3850	0.0827	0.0807	19	
	20	2.6533	0.3769	12.4622	12.7712	0.0802	0.0783	20	
	21	2.7860	0.3589	12.8212	13.1391	0.0780	0.0761	21	
	22	2.9253	0.3418	13.1630	13.4894	0.0760	0.0741	22	
	23	3.0715	0.3256	13.4886	13.8230	0.0741	0.0723	23	
	24	3.2251	0.3101	13.7986	14.1408	0.0725	0.0707	24	
	25	3.3864	0.2953	14.0939	14.4434	0.0710	0.0692	25	
	1	1.0600	0.9434	0.9434	0.9714	1.0600	1.0294	1	
	2	1.1236	0.8900	1.8334	1.8879	0.5454	0.5297	2	
	3	1.1910	0.8396	2.6730	2.7524	0.3741	0.3633	3	
	4	1.2626	0.7921	3.4651	3.5680	0.2886	0.2803	4	
	5	1.3382	0.7473	4.2124	4.3375	0.2374	0.2305	5	
	6	1.4185	0.7050	4.9173	5.0634	0.2034	0.1975	6	
	7	1.5036	0.6651	5.5824	5.7482	0.1791	1.1740	7	
	8	1.5938	0.6274	6.2098	6.3943	0.160	0.1564	8	
	9	1.6895	0.5919	6.8017	7.0038	0.1470	0.1428	9	
	10	1.7908	0.5584	7.3601	7.5787	0.1359	0.1319	10	
	11	1.8983	0.5268	7.8869	8.1212	0.1268	0.1231	11	
6.0%	12	2.0122	0.4970	8.3838	8.6329	0.1193	0.1158	12	6.0%
	13	2.1329	0.4688	8.8527	9.1157	0.1130	0.1097	13	
	14	2.2609	0.4423	9.2950	9.5711	0.1076	0.1045	14	
	15	2.3966	0.4173	9.7122	10.0008	0.1030	0.1000	15	
	16	2.5404	0.3936	10.1059	10.4061	0.0990	0.0961	16	
	17	2.6928	0.3714	10.4773	10.7885	0.0954	0.0927	17	
	18	2.8543	0.3503	10.8276	11.1493	0.0924	0.0897	18	
	19	3.0256	0.3305	11.1581	11.4896	0.0896	0.0870	19	
	20	3.2071	0.3118	11.4699	11.8107	0.0872	0.0847	20	
	21	3.3996	0.2942	11.7641	12.1136	0.0850	0.0826	21	
	22	3.6035	0.2775	12.0416	12.3993	0.0830	0.0806	22	
	23	3.8197	0.2618	12.3034	12.6689	0.0813	0.0789	23	
	24	4.0489	0.2470	12.5504	12.9232	0.0797	0.0774	24	
	25	4.2919	0.2330	12.7834	13.1631	0.0782	0.0760	25	

	Year	Amount to which £1 will accumulate	Present value of £1	Present value of £1 received at end of period	Present value of £1 received continuously	Amount received at end of year which will recover initial investment of £1	Amount received at end of year which will recover initial investment of £1	Year	
	1	1.0700	0.9346	0.9346	0.9669	1.0700	1.0342	1	
	2	1.1449	0.8734	1.8080	1.8706	0.5531	0.5346	2	
	3	1.2250	0.8163	2.6243	2.7151	0.3811	0.3683	3	
	4	1.3108	0.7629	3.3872	3.5044	0.2952	0.2854	4	
	5	1.4026	0.7130	4.1002	4.2421	0.2439	0.2357	5	
	6	1.5007	0.6663	4.7665	4.9316	0.2098	0.2028	6	
	7	1.6058	0.6227	5.3893	5.5758	0.1856	0.1793	7	
	8	1.7182	0.5820	5.9713	6.1779	0.1675	0.1619	8	
	9	1.8385	0.5439	6.5152	6.7407	0.1535	0.1484	9	
	10	1.9672	0.5083	7.0236	7.2666	0.1424	0.1376	10	
	11	2.1049	0.4751	7.4987	7.7582	0.1334	0.1289	11	
7.0%	12	2.2522	0.4440	7.9427	8.2175	0.1259	0.1217	12	7.0%
	13	2.4098	0.4150	8.3577	8.6469	0.1197	0.1156	13	
	14	2.5785	0.3878	8.7455	9.0481	0.1143	0.1105	14	
	15	2.7590	0.3624	9.1079	9.4231	0.1098	0.1061	15	
	16	2.9522	0.3387	9.4466	9.7736	0.1059	0.1023	16	
	17	3.1588	0.3166	9.7632	10.1011	0.1024	0.0990	17	
	18	3.3799	0.2959	10.0591	10.4072	0.0994	0.0961	18	
	19	3.6165	0.2765	10.3356	10.6933	0.0968	0.0935	19	
	20	3.8697	0.2584	10.5940	10.9606	0.0944	0.0912	20	
	21	4.1406	0.2415	10.8355	11.2105	0.0923	0.0892	21	
	22	4.4304	0.2257	11.0612	11.4440	0.0904	0.0874	22	
	23	4.7405	0.2109	11.2722	11.6623	0.0887	0.0857	23	
	24	5.0724	0.1971	11.4693	11.8662	0.0872	0.0843	24	
	25	5.4274	0.1842	11.6536	12.0569	0.0858	0.0829	25	
	1	1.0800	0.9259	0.9259	0.9625	1.0800	1.0390	1	
	2	1.1664	0.8573	1.7833	1.8537	0.5608	0.5395	2	
	3	1.2597	0.7938	2.5771	2.6789	0.3880	0.3733	3	
	4	1.3605	0.7350	3.3121	3.4429	0.3019	0.2905	4	
	5	1.4693	0.6806	3.9927	4.1504	0.2505	0.2409	5	
	6	1.5869	0.6302	4.6229	4.8054	0.2163	0.2081	6	
	7	1.7138	0.5835	5.2064	5.4120	0.1921	0.1848	7	
	8	1.8509	0.5403	5.7466	5.9736	0.1740	0.1674	8	
	9	1.9990	0.5002	6.2469	6.4936	0.1601	0.1540	9	
	10	2.1589	0.4632	6.7101	6.9750	0.1490	0.1434	10	
	11	2.3316	0.4289	7.1390	7.4209	0.1401	0.1348	11	
8.0%	12	2.5182	0.3971	7.5361	7.8337	0.1327	0.1277	12	8.0%
	13	2.7196	0.3677	7.9038	8.2159	0.1265	0.1217	13	
	14	2.9372	0.3405	8.2442	8.5698	0.1213	0.1167	14	
	15	3.1722	0.3152	8.5595	8.8975	0.1168	0.1124	15	
	16	3.4259	0.2919	8.8514	9.2009	0.1130	0.1087	16	
	17	3.7000	0.2703	9.1216	9.4818	0.1096	0.1055	17	
	18	3.9960	0.2502	9.3719	9.7420	0.1067	0.1026	18	
	19	4.3157	0.2317	9.6036	9.9828	0.1041	0.1002	19	
	20	4.6610	0.2145	9.8181	10.2058	0.1019	0.0980	20	
	21	5.0338	0.1987	10.0168	10.4123	0.0998	0.0960	21	
	22	5.4365	0.1839	10.2007	10.6035	0.0980	0.0943	22	
	23	5.8715	0.1703	10.3711	10.7806	0.0964	0.0928	23	
	24	6.3412	0.1577	10.5288	10.9445	0.0950	0.0914	24	
	25	6.8485	0.1460	10.6748	11.0963	0.0937	0.0901	25	

Year	Amount to which £1 will accumulate	Present value of £1	Present value of £1 received at end of period	Present value of £1 received continuously	Amount received at end of year which will recover initial investment of £1	Amount received at end of year which will recover initial investment of £1	Year	
	1	1.0900	0.9174	0.9174	0.9581	1.0900	1.0437	1	
	2	1.1881	0.8417	1.7591	1.8371	0.5685	0.5443	2	
	3	1.2950	0.7722	2.5313	2.6436	0.3951	0.3783	3	
	4	1.4116	0.7084	3.2397	3.3834	0.3087	0.2956	4	
	5	1.5386	0.6499	3.8897	4.0622	0.2571	0.2462	5	
	6	1.6771	0.5963	4.4859	4.6849	0.2229	0.2135	6	
	7	1.8280	0.5470	5.0330	5.2562	0.1987	0.1903	7	
	8	1.9926	0.5019	5.5348	5.7803	0.1807	0.1730	8	
	9	2.1719	0.4604	5.9952	6.2612	0.1668	0.1597	9	
	10	2.3674	0.4224	6.4177	6.7023	0.1558	0.1492	10	
	11	2.5804	0.3875	6.8052	7.1070	0.1469	0.1407	11	
9.0%	12	2.8127	0.3555	7.1607	7.4783	0.1397	0.1337	12	9.0%
	13	3.0658	0.3262	7.4869	7.8190	0.1336	0.1279	13	
	14	3.3417	0.2992	7.7862	8.1315	0.1284	0.1230	14	
	15	3.6425	0.2745	8.0607	8.4182	0.1241	0.1188	15	
	16	3.9703	0.2519	8.3126	8.6813	0.1203	0.1152	16	
	17	4.3276	0.2311	8.5436	8.9226	0.1170	0.1121	17	
	18	4.7171	0.2120	8.7556	9.1440	0.1142	0.1094	18	
	19	5.1417	0.1945	8.9501	9.3471	0.1117	0.1070	19	
	20	5.6044	0.1784	9.1285	9.5334	0.1095	0.1049	20	
	21	6.1088	0.1637	9.2922	9.7044	0.1076	0.1030	21	
	22	6.6586	0.1502	9.4424	9.8612	0.1059	0.1014	22	
	23	7.2579	0.1378	9.5802	10.0051	0.1044	0.0999	23	
	24	7.9111	0.1264	9.7066	10.1371	0.1030	0.0986	24	
	25	8.6231	0.1160	9.8226	10.2582	0.1018	0.0975	25	
	1	1.1000	0.9091	0.9091	0.9538	1.1000	1.0484	1	
	2	1.2100	0.8264	1.7355	1.8209	0.5762	0.5492	2	
	3	1.3310	0.7513	2.4869	2.6092	0.4021	0.3833	3	
	4	1.4641	0.6830	3.1699	3.3258	0.3155	0.3007	4	
	5	1.6105	0.6209	3.7908	3.9773	0.2638	0.2514	5	
	6	1.7716	0.5645	4.3553	4.5694	0.2296	0.2188	6	
	7	1.9487	0.5132	4.8684	5.1080	0.2054	0.1958	7	
	8	2.1436	0.4665	5.3349	5.5974	0.1874	0.1787	8	
	9	2.3579	0.4241	5.7590	6.0424	0.1736	0.1655	9	
	10	2.5937	0.3855	6.1446	6.4469	0.1627	0.1551	10	
	11	2.8531	0.3505	6.4951	6.8147	0.1540	0.1467	11	
10.0%	12	3.1384	0.3186	6.8137	7.1490	0.1468	0.1399	12	10.0%
	13	3.4523	0.2897	7.1034	7.4529	0.1408	0.1342	13	
	14	3.7975	0.2633	7.3667	7.7292	0.1357	0.1294	14	
	15	4.1772	0.2394	7.6061	7.9803	0.1315	0.1253	15	
	16	4.5950	0.2176	7.8237	8.2087	0.1278	0.1218	16	
	17	5.0545	0.1978	8.0216	8.4163	0.1247	0.1188	17	
	18	5.5599	0.1799	8.2014	8.6050	0.1219	0.1162	18	
	19	6.1159	0.1635	8.3649	8.7765	0.1195	0.1139	19	
	20	6.7275	0.1486	8.5136	8.9325	0.1175	0.1120	20	
	21	7.4002	0.1351	8.6487	9.0743	0.1156	0.1102	21	
	22	8.1403	0.1228	8.7715	9.2032	0.1140	0.1087	22	
	23	8.9543	0.1117	8.8832	9.3203	0.1126	0.1073	23	
	24	9.8497	0.1015	8.9847	9.4268	0.1113	0.1061	24	
	25	10.8347	0.0923	9.0770	9.5237	0.1102	0.1050	25	

Year	Amount to which £1 will accumulate	Present value of £1	Present value of £1 received at end of period	Present value of £1 received continuously	Amount received at end of year which will recover initial investment of £1	Amount received at end of year which will recover initial investment of £1	Year
1	1.1100	0.9009	0.9009	0.9496	1.1100	1.0531	1
2	1.2321	0.8116	1.7125	1.8051	0.5839	0.5540	2
3	1.3676	0.7312	2.4437	2.5758	0.4092	0.3882	3
4	1.5181	0.6587	3.1024	3.2701	0.3223	0.3058	4
5	1.6851	0.5935	3.6959	3.8956	0.2706	0.2567	5
6	1.8704	0.5346	4.2305	4.4592	0.2364	0.2243	6
7	2.0762	0.4817	4.7122	4.9669	0.2122	0.2013	7
8	2.3045	0.4339	5.1461	5.4242	0.1943	0.1844	8
9	2.5580	0.3909	5.5370	5.8363	0.1806	0.1713	9
10	2.8394	0.3522	5.8892	6.2075	0.1698	0.1611	10
11	3.1518	0.3173	6.2065	6.5419	0.1611	0.1529	11
11.0% 12	3.4985	0.2858	6.4924	6.8432	0.1540	0.1461	12 11.0%
13	3.8833	0.2575	6.7499	7.1147	0.1482	0.1406	13
14	4.3104	0.2320	6.9819	7.3592	0.1432	0.1359	14
15	4.7846	0.2090	7.1909	7.5795	0.1391	0.1319	15
16	5.3105	0.1883	7.3792	7.7780	0.1355	0.1286	16
17	5.8951	0.1696	7.5488	7.9568	0.1325	0.1257	17
18	6.5436	0.1528	7.7016	8.1178	0.1298	0.1232	18
19	7.2633	0.1377	7.8393	8.2630	0.1276	0.1210	19
20	8.0623	0.1240	7.9633	8.3937	0.1256	0.1191	20
21	8.9492	0.1117	8.0751	8.5115	0.1238	0.1175	21
22	9.9336	0.1007	8.1757	8.6176	0.1223	0.1160	22
23	11.0263	0.0907	8.2664	8.7132	0.1210	0.1148	23
24	12.2392	0.0817	8.3481	8.7993	0.1198	0.1136	24
25	13.5855	0.0736	8.4217	8.8769	0.1187	0.1127	25
1	1.1200	0.8929	0.8929	0.9454	1.1200	1.0577	1
2	1.2544	0.7972	1.6901	1.7895	0.5917	0.5558	2
3	1.4049	0.7118	2.4018	2.5432	0.4163	0.3932	3
4	1.5735	0.6355	3.0373	3.2161	0.3292	0.3109	4
5	1.7623	0.5674	3.6048	3.8170	0.2774	0.2620	5
6	1.9738	0.5066	4.1114	4.3534	0.2432	0.2297	6
7	2.2107	0.4523	4.5638	4.8324	0.2191	0.2069	7
8	2.4760	0.4039	4.9676	5.2601	0.2013	0.1901	8
9	2.7731	0.3606	5.3282	5.6419	0.1877	0.1772	9
10	3.1058	0.3220	5.6502	5.9828	0.1770	0.1671	10
11	3.4785	0.2876	5.9377	6.2872	0.1684	0.1591	11
12.0% 12	3.8960	0.2567	6.1944	6.5590	0.1614	0.1525	12 12.0%
13	4.3636	0.2292	6.4235	6.8017	0.1557	0.1470	13
14	4.8871	0.2046	6.6282	7.0183	0.1509	0.1425	14
15	5.4736	0.1827	6.8109	7.2118	0.1468	0.1387	15
16	6.1304	0.1631	6.9740	7.3845	0.1434	0.1354	16
17	6.8660	0.1456	7.1196	7.5387	0.1405	0.1326	17
18	7.6900	0.1300	7.2497	7.6764	0.1379	0.1303	18
19	8.6128	0.1161	7.3658	7.7994	0.1358	0.1282	19
20	9.6463	0.1037	7.4694	7.9091	0.1339	0.1264	20
21	10.8038	0.0926	7.5620	8.0072	0.1322	0.1269	21
22	12.1003	0.0826	7.6446	8.0947	0.1308	0.1235	22
23	13.5523	0.0738	7.7184	8.1728	0.1296	0.1224	23
24	15.1786	0.0659	7.7843	8.2426	0.1285	0.1213	24
25	17.001	0.0588	7.8431	8.3048	0.1275	0.1204	25

	Year	Amount to which £1 will accumulate	Present value of £1	Present value of £1 received at end of period	Present value of £1 received continuously	Amount received at end of year which will recover initial investment of £1	Amount received at end of year which will recover initial investment of £1	Year	
	1	1.1300	0.8850	0.8850	0.9413	1.1300	1.0624	1	
	2	1.2769	0.7831	1.6681	1.7743	0.5995	0.5636	2	
	3	1.4429	0.6931	2.3612	2.5115	0.4236	0.3982	3	
	4	1.6305	0.6133	2.9745	3.1639	0.3362	0.3161	4	
	5	1.8424	0.5428	3.5172	3.7412	0.2843	0.2673	5	
	6	2.0820	0.4803	3.9975	4.2521	0.2602	0.2352	6	
	7	2.3526	0.4251	4.4226	4.7042	0.2261	0.2126	7	
	8	2.6584	0.3762	4.7988	5.1043	0.2084	0.1959	8	
	9	3.0040	0.3329	5.1317	5.4584	0.1949	0.1832	9	
	10	3.3946	0.2946	5.4262	5.7718	0.1843	0.1733	10	
	11	3.8359	0.2607	5.6869	6.0491	0.1758	0.1653	11	
13.0%	12	4.3345	0.2307	5.9176	6.2945	0.1690	0.1589	12	13.0%
	13	4.8980	0.2042	6.1218	6.5116	0.1634	0.1526	13	
	14	5.5348	0.1807	6.3025	6.7038	0.1587	0.1492	14	
	15	6.2543	0.1599	6.4624	6.8739	0.1547	0.1455	15	
	16	7.0673	0.1415	6.6039	7.0244	0.1514	0.1424	16	
	17	7.9861	0.1252	6.7291	7.1576	0.1486	0.1397	17	
	18	9.0243	0.1108	6.8399	7.2754	0.1462	0.1374	18	
	19	10.1974	0.0981	6.9380	7.3798	0.1441	0.1355	19	
	20	11.5231	0.0868	7.0248	7.4721	0.1424	0.1338	20	
	21	13.0211	0.0768	7.1016	7.5538	0.1408	0.1324	21	
	22	14.7138	0.0680	7.1695	7.6260	0.1395	0.1311	22	
	23	16.6266	0.0601	7.2297	7.6900	0.1383	0.1300	23	
	24	18.7881	0.0532	7.2829	7.7466	0.1373	0.1291	24	
	25	21.2305	0.0471	7.3300	7.7967	0.1364	0.1283	25	
	1	1.1400	0.8772	0.8772	0.9373	1.1400	1.0669	1	
	2	1.2996	0.7695	1.6467	1.7594	0.6073	0.5684	2	
	3	1.4815	0.6750	2.3216	2.4806	0.4307	0.4031	3	
	4	1.6890	0.6921	2.9137	3.1132	0.3432	0.3212	4	
	5	1.9254	0.5194	3.4331	3.6682	0.2913	0.2726	5	
	6	2.1950	0.4556	3.8887	4.1549	0.2572	0.2407	6	
	7	2.5023	0.3996	4.2883	4.5819	0.2332	0.2182	7	
	8	2.8526	0.3506	4.6389	4.9565	0.2156	0.2018	8	
	9	3.2519	0.3075	4.9464	5.2851	0.2022	0.1892	9	
	10	3.7072	0.2697	5.2161	5.5733	0.1917	0.1794	10	
	11	4.2262	0.2366	5.4527	5.8261	0.1834	0.1716	11	
14.0%	12	4.8179	0.2076	5.6603	6.0479	0.1767	0.1653	12	14.0%
	13	5.4924	0.1821	5.8424	6.2424	0.1713	0.1602	13	
	14	6.2613	0.1597	6.0021	6.4130	0.1666	0.1559	14	
	15	7.1379	0.1401	6.1422	6.5627	0.1628	0.1524	15	
	16	8.1372	0.1229	6.2651	6.6940	0.1596	0.1494	16	
	17	9.2765	0.1078	6.3729	6.8092	0.1569	0.1469	17	
	18	10.5752	0.0946	6.4674	6.9103	0.1546	0.1447	18	
	19	12,0557	0.0829	6.5504	6.9989	0.1527	0.1429	19	
	20	13.7435	0.0728	6.6231	7.0766	0.1510	0.1413	20	
	21	15.6676	0.0638	6.6870	7.1448	0.1496	0.1400	21	
	22	17.8610	0.0560	6.7429	7.2046	0.1483	0.1388	22	
	23	20.3616	0.0491	6.7921	7.2571	0.1472	0.1378	23	
	24	23.2122	0.0431	6.8351	7.3032	0.1463	0.1369	24	
	25	26.4619	0.0378	6.8729	7.3435	0.1455	0.1362	25	

Year	Amount to which £1 will accumulate	Present value of £1	Present value of £1 received at end of period	Present value of £1 received continuously	Amount received at end of year which will recover initial investment of £1	Amount received at end of year which will recover initial investment of £1	Year
1	1.1500	0.8696	0.8696	0.9333	1.1500	1.0715	1
2	1.3225	0.7561	1.6257	1.7448	0.6151	0.5731	2
3	1.5209	0.6575	2.2832	2.4505	0.4380	0.4081	3
4	1.7490	0.5718	2.8550	3.0641	0.3503	0.3264	4
5	2.0114	0.4972	3.3522	3.5977	0.2983	0.2780	5
6	2.3131	0.4323	3.7845	4.0617	0.2642	0.2462	6
7	2.6600	0.3759	4.1604	4.4652	0.2404	0.2240	7
8	3.0590	0.3269	4.4873	4.8160	0.2229	0.2076	8
9	3.5179	0.2843	4.7716	5.1211	0.2096	0.1953	9
10	4.0456	0.2472	5.0188	5.3864	0.1993	0.1857	10
11	4.6524	0.2149	5.2337	5.6171	0.1911	0.1780	11
12	5.3503	0.1869	5.4206	5.8177	0.1845	0.1719	12
13	6.1528	0.1625	5.5831	5.9921	0.1791	0.1669	13
14	7.0757	0.1413	5.7245	6.1438	0.1747	0.1628	14
15	8.1371	0.1229	5.8474	6.2757	0.1710	0.1593	15
16	9.3576	0.1069	5.9542	6.3904	0.1679	0.1565	16
17	10.7613	0.0929	6.0472	6.4901	0.1654	0.1541	17
18	12.3755	0.0808	6.1280	6.5769	0.1632	0.1520	18
19	14.2318	0.0703	6.1982	6.6523	0.1613	0.1503	19
20	16.3665	0.0611	6.2593	6.7178	0.1598	0.1489	20
21	18.8215	0.0531	6.3126	6.7749	0.1584	0.1476	21
22	21.6447	0.0462	6.3587	6.8245	0.1573	0.1465	22
23	24.8915	0.0402	6.3988	6.8676	0.1563	0.1456	23
24	28.6252	0.0349	6.4338	6.9051	0.1554	0.1448	24
25	32.9190	0.0304	6.4641	6.9377	0.1547	0.1441	25
1	1.1600	0.8621	0.8621	0.9293	1.1600	1.0760	1
2	1.3456	0.7432	1.6052	1.7305	0.6230	0.5779	2
3	1.5609	0.6407	2.2459	2.4211	0.4453	0.4130	3
4	1.8106	0.5523	2.7982	3.0165	0.3574	0.3315	4
5	2.1003	0.4761	3.2743	3.5298	0.3054	0.2833	5
6	2.4364	0.4104	3.6847	3.9722	0.2714	0.2517	6
7	2.8262	0.3538	4.0386	4.3537	0.2476	0.2297	7
8	3.2784	0.3050	4.3436	4.6825	0.2302	0.2136	8
9	3.8030	0.2630	4.6065	4.9660	0.2171	0.2014	9
10	4.4114	0.2267	4.8332	5.2103	0.2089	0.1919	10
11	5.1173	0.1954	5.0286	5.4210	0.1989	0.1845	11
12	5.9360	0.1685	5.1971	5.6026	0.1924	0.1785	12
13	6.8858	0.1452	5.3423	5.7592	0.1872	0.1736	13
14	7.9875	0.1252	5.4675	5.8941	0.1829	0.1697	14
15	9.2655	0.1070	5.5755	6.0105	0.1794	0.1664	15
16	10.7480	0.0930	5.6685	6.1108	0.1764	0.1636	16
17	12.4677	0.0802	5.7487	6.1972	0.1740	0.1614	17
18	14.4625	0.0691	5.8178	6.2718	0.1719	0.1594	18
19	16.7765	0.0596	5.8775	6.3360	0.1701	0.1578	19
20	19.4608	0.0514	5.9288	6.3914	0.1687	0.1565	20
21	22.5745	0.0443	5.9731	6.4392	0.1674	0.1553	21
22	26.1864	0.0382	6.0113	6.4803	0.1664	0.1543	22
23	30.3762	0.0329	6.0442	6.5158	0.1654	0.1535	23
24	35.2364	0.0284	6.0726	6.5464	0.1647	0.1528	24
25	40.8742	0.0245	6.0971	6.5728	0.1640	0.1521	25

15.0% (years 1–25), 16.0% (years 1–25)

INDEX